Vision *from the* Inner Eye

Vision *from the* Inner Eye

*The Photographic Art
of
A L Syed*

O P Sharma

Mapin Publishing, Ahmedabad

The publication of this book has been made possible
with a generous grant from
B Arunkumar Capital & Credit Services Pvt. Ltd., Mumbai

First published in India
in 2001 by
Mapin Publishing Pvt. Ltd.
Ahmedabad 380013 INDIA
www.mapinpub.com

Simultaneously published in the United States of America
in 2001 by
Grantha Corporation
80 Cliffedgeway, Middletown, NJ 07701

Distributed in North America by
Antique Collectors' Club
Market Street Industrial Park
Wappingers' Falls, NY 12590
Tel: 800-252-5321 • Fax: 914-297-0068
www.antiquecc.com

Distributed in United Kingdom & Europe by
Antique Collectors' Club
5 Church Street, Woodbridge
Suffolk IP12 1DS
Tel: 1394-385-501 • Fax: 1394-384-434
email: accvs@aol.com

Distributed in Asia by
International Publishers Direct (S) Pte. Ltd.
240 Macpherson Road
#08-01 Pines International Building
Singapore 348574
Tel: 65-7416933 • Fax: 65-7416922
email: ipdsing@singnet.com.sg

ISBN: 1-890206-28-8 (Grantha)
ISBN: 81-85822-81-6 (Mapin)
LC: 00-13561

Text © O P Sharma & Azmat A Syed
Photographs © Azmat A Syed
Editor: Christina Sullivan Sarabhai
Designed by: Paulomi Shah/Mapin Design Studio
Colour Separations & Printed by: Tien Wah Press, Singapore

Captions:

Jacket

Front: Study corner, Rajasthan

Back (clockwise from top left):
• Silent corner, Palanpur tomb
• Difficult climb, Jaisalmer
• Before they catch me, Palanpur
• *Poojari,* priest

Opposite: A L Syed in his last days

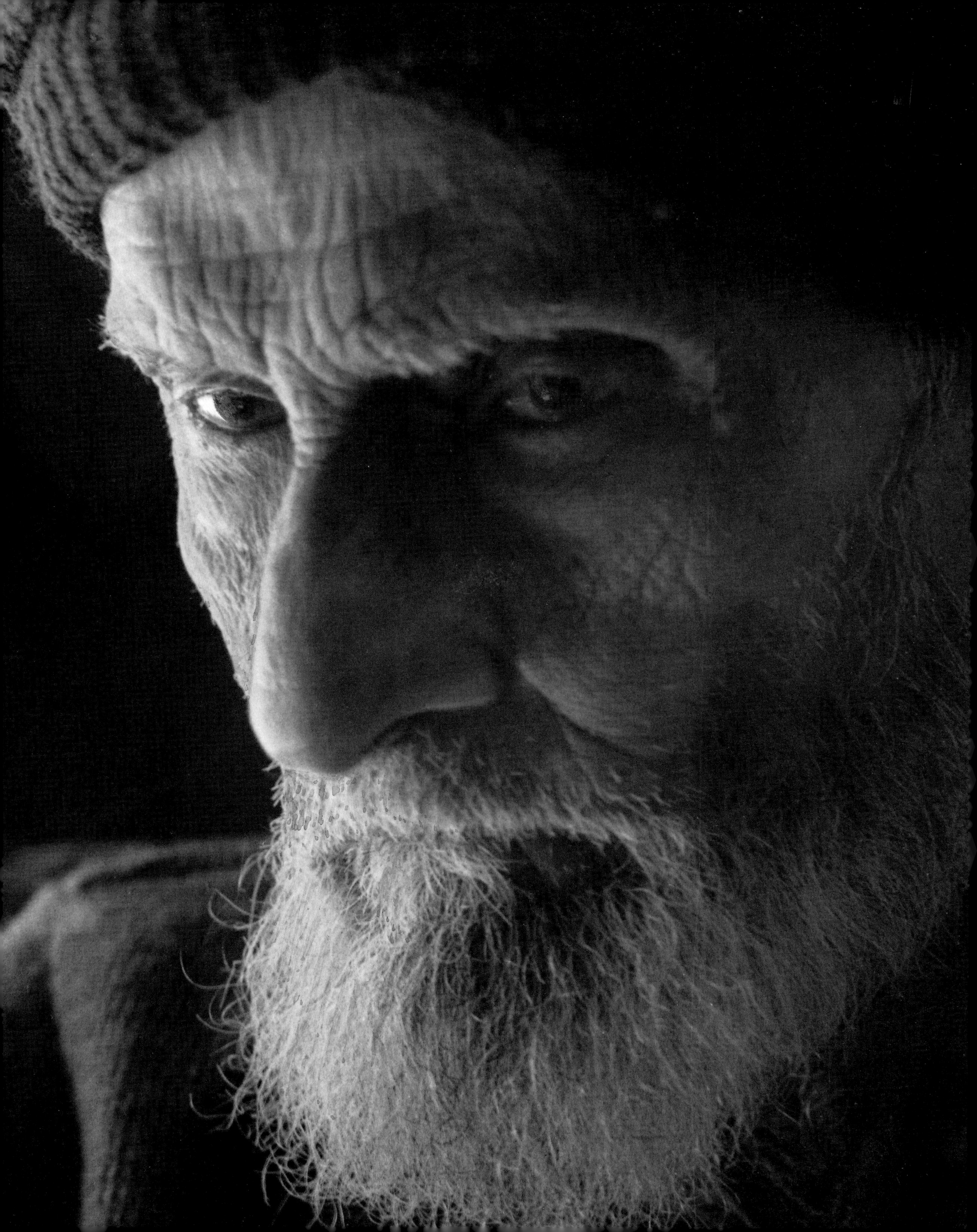

Foreword

I feel proud and privileged to have been requested by Azmatbhai to write the text for this unique book on his father, one of the most important personalities in the world of Indian photography of this century, the late Janab A L Syed.

To sum up a lifetime of work in just a few pages seems like an impossible task. In my humble way I have tried to pay my respects to the grand old master of the photographic world. I hope those who knew him and his work will forgive me if I have omitted any phase of his life or his work that should have been included.

It is very unfortunate that many negatives of his unforgettable pictures are either in a deteriorated condition or untraceable. The royal families themselves and collectors abroad, especially after Independence, have acquired much of the work he and his brother K L Syed produced during the princely era in pre-Independence India. Similarly, his work in the film world has become the property of the producers. Hence, out of necessity a number of pictures in this book have been reproduced from copy negatives which do not match the quality of the original.

Words are not enough to describe Janab A L Syed's photographic achievements, his aesthetic sense, technical excellence, keen vision, sense of composition and complete mastery over the medium. We only wish that this book had been published when he was in the prime of his photographic career. It would have brought happiness to a soul who devoted his entire life to the art of photography and its advancement.

We hope that this book will provide some insights to the younger generation of aspiring photographers about his significant contribution to the world of photography.

O P Sharma
Founder and Hon. General Secretary
India International Photographic Council, New Delhi

Acknowledgements

It is with tremendous gratitude that I acknowledge all those who have helped, guided and inspired me to bring out this book. I am especially grateful to: the late Nawab Tale Mohamed Khan of Palanpur for patronising and encouraging the entire Syed family in all possible ways to pursue photography; the present Nawab sahib Iqbal Mohamed Khan of Palanpur, whose support and guidance made my dream of bringing out this book a reality; and my brothers Akhtar Syed, Asad Syed and Sabbir Syed for their keen encouragement and for providing me with all the necessary information.

I would like to thank Shri N A Bharati, Shri S S Sharma, Shrimati Chitrangada Sharma and Shri O P Sharma for their help in preparing the manuscript.

I am also grateful to H H Maharao Brijraj Singhji of Kotah; H H Maharawal Mahipal Singhji of Dungarpur; Rajmata Sushila Kumariji of Bikaner; Shri B K Gadhvi of Palanpur; Shri Kishore Mehta of Bombay; Dr. B T Trivedi of Palanpur; Shri Sanat Shukla of *The Times of India*; Shri P N Mehra of Delhi; Shri T Kasinath of Delhi; Shri Sabbir K Syed of Syed Photographers, Palanpur; and Shri B S Sodhi of Ambala, who wrote for this book heartfelt tributes in remembrance of my father.

Azmat A Syed
Palanpur

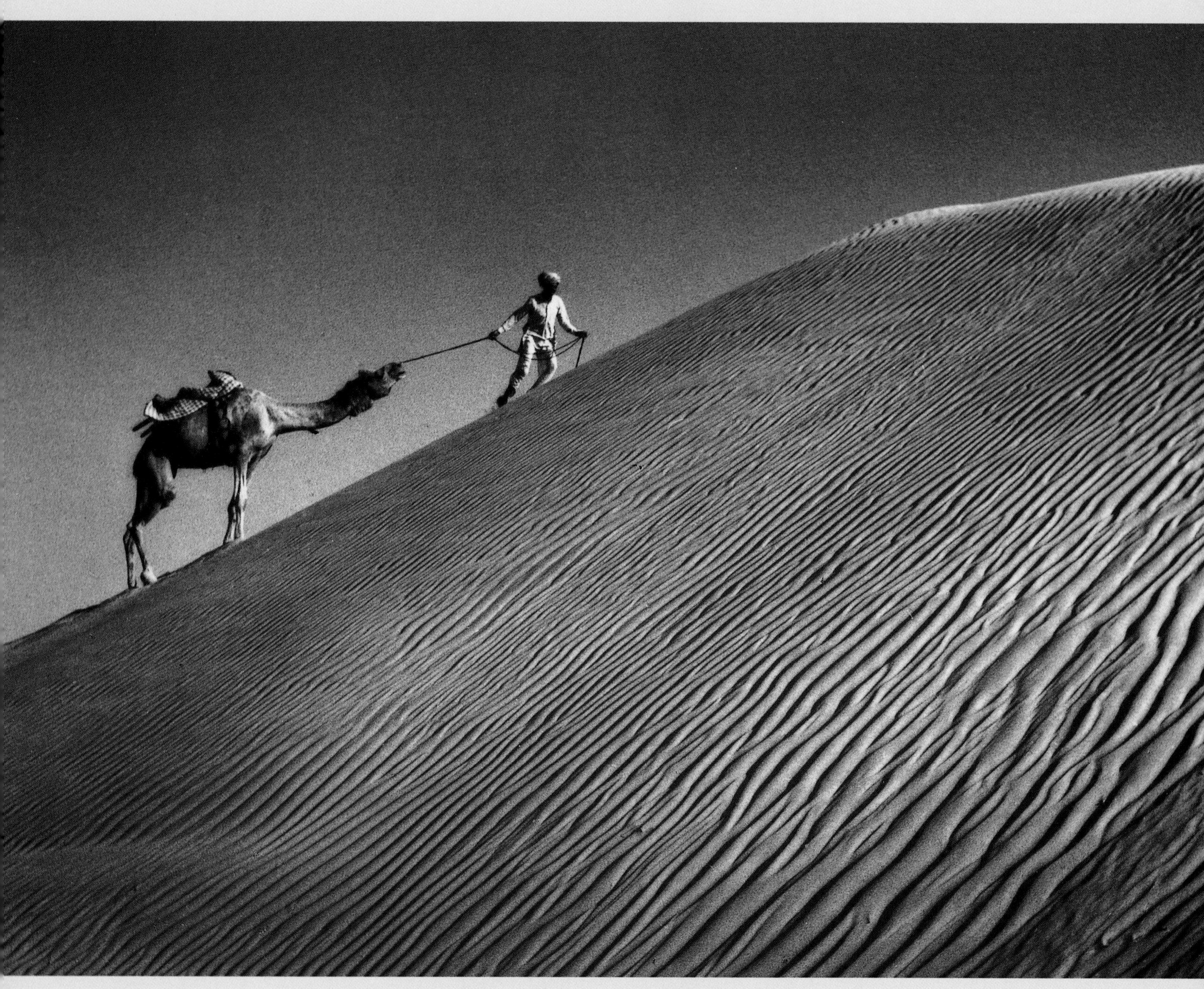

Difficult climb, Jaisalmer

Introduction

The period preceding Independence in India is known as the princely era, as Maharajas, Nawabs and princes ruled various independent states. During this time, many of the early photographers ran studios for portraiture and for covering social and other functions held by royalty. Although the number of photographers gradually increased, very few had the passion and flair for photography which A L Syed possessed. He built a 70-year career on the magical combination of an artist's eye and the technical skill necessary to compose affecting images. He will always be remembered for this exceptional skill and his lifelong sincere devotion to photography.

Abid Mian Lal Mian Syed (A L Syed) was born in 1904 in Varnawada, a small village in Banaskantha district, Gujarat, and he spent his childhood in nearby Palanpur. His father Janab Lal Mian Syed was a well-known Unani hakim and a courtier of the late Nawab Tale Mohamed Khan of Palanpur.

A L Syed studied in the government high school but did not perform well academically. His father wanted him to be a hakim like himself but his destiny lay elsewhere. At the age of 15, he started working with his elder brother Janab Khanji Mian Lal Mian Syed (K L Syed), who was already a well-known freelance photographer in Palanpur, particularly for portraiture.

In 1923 on a trip to Bombay to clear his matriculation examination, he took a photograph of the sunrise at Chowpaty, which won him first prize in *The Illustrated Weekly of India* Photo Contest. This decisive experience hooked young Abid as a photographer.

In course of time, under his brother's guidance and loving care, A L Syed joined him as official photographer of Palanpur state. Through their association with the royal family, their reputation grew and they were often requested to photograph royal families of other states: Baroda and Saurashtra (in what is now Gujarat), Bikaner, Kotah, Jodhpur, Udaipur, Bundi, Dungarpur and Narsinghgarh (in what is now Rajasthan), Madhya Pradesh and Kashmir.

A L Syed came to be one of the most loved state photographers for his superior skill, manners and professionalism. He was a charming young man whose enthusiasm and humility earned him great respect. Among royalty he was always treated as a member of the family and had unusually close proximity to the family members, including the women who were traditionally in purdah. He took innumerable photographs with his unique flair and style, which are now considered to be historical documentation of the pomp and pageantry of royal living, especially hunting expeditions, weddings and other functions.

In 1946 A L Syed accompanied the Nawab of Palanpur when he moved to Bombay, and he lived and worked there until 1975, travelling back and forth to Palanpur every month to see his wife and children.

Unlike his brother who restricted himself to state photography, from his early days A L Syed was determined to take excellent photographs wherever and whenever possible. During his travels around the country, both on official assignments with the Nawabs as well as independently, he was always alert and aware of his surroundings. In fact, while spending time with him, one often felt that his zeal to discover the potential photograph consumed a great deal of his attention. He had an uncanny knack of spotting his subject; his eyes, mind and fingers worked in perfect synchronisation to instantly capture remarkable images through his lens. He always said that opportunities in photography never wait for anyone and "the one who is armed at all times gets home with a camera full of good pictures."

He however did not wait to go home to develop the exposures. Instead he would rush to the nearest photo lab. His product proved that he never missed the moment and always produced astonishing results. Propelled by the desire to see his photographs in print, he would approach various publications, all of which were thrilled to publish his work.

In 1925 his images first began to appear regularly in *Kumar*, a monthly Gujarati magazine edited by the great artist Ravi Shankar Raval. A L Syed also wrote monthly feature articles on the subject of photography to accompany his photographs, which continued until the magazine ceased publication in 1940. From 1930 to 1980 his

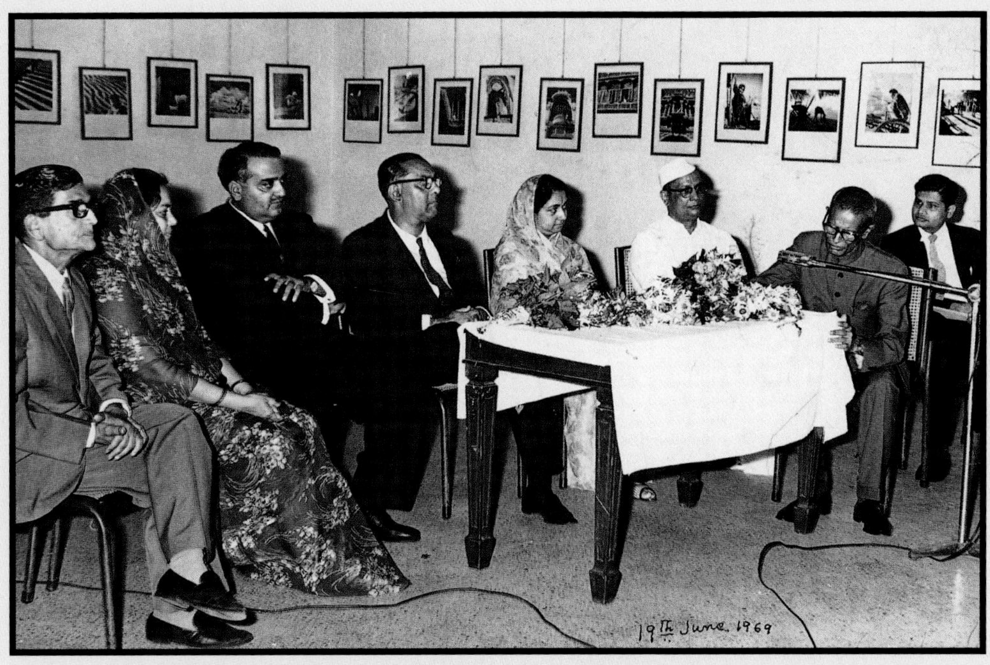

Group photo, one-man show, 1969

work also appeared regularly in *The Illustrated Weekly of India*. Eventually he became the only photographer who could justly claim that there was no publication in India that had not published his photographs.

Around 1930 he also started exhibiting his photographs in salons and other national and international exhibitions and competitions. He was the first Indian to dramatically gatecrash into the international scene when his famous photograph Traveller of the East was published in the *World's Best Photographs* compiled by Odhams Press. This haunting picture was exhibited in over 40 international salons and won the Popular Photography award in 1935 and later was purchased for the famous Hutchinson collection in the USA.

That same year, Mr. Baker, the General Manager of the Kodak Co., Bombay, requested Abid to take some photographs with a Brownie Box Camera. He accepted the challenge and a dozen enlargements were displayed for a month in the Kodak shop windows.

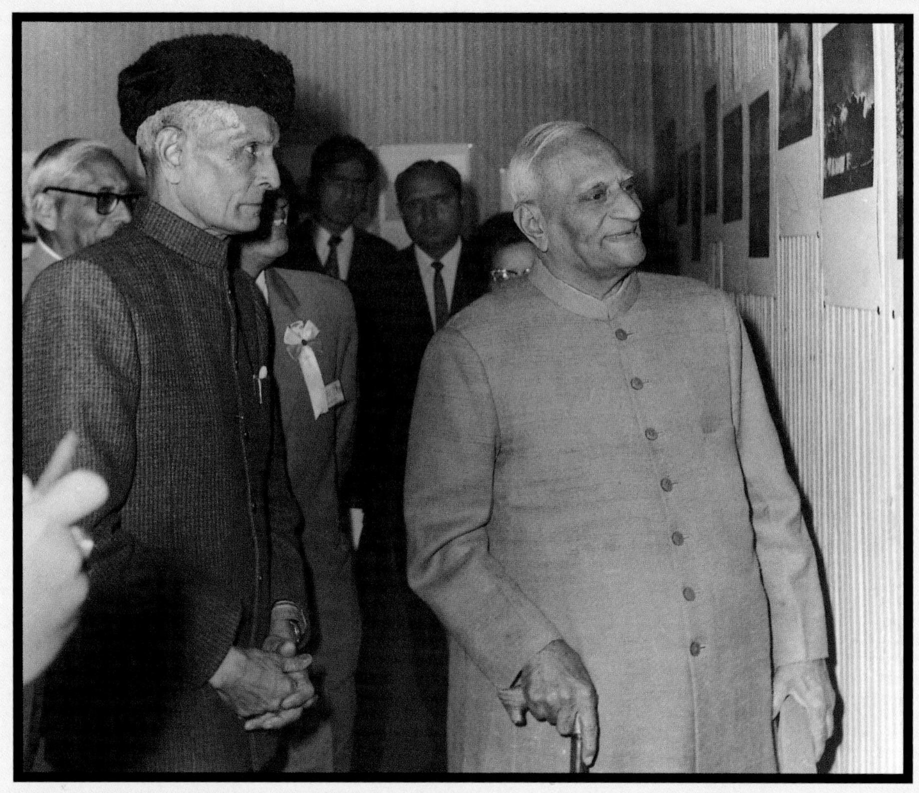

With Shri V V Giri, President of India, right, 1973

During the next 50 years he won countless awards and many photographic societies, clubs and cultural organisations conferred honours on him. He was one of the most respected and sought-after judges in salons and contests.

In 1973 one of his numerous one-man shows was inaugurated by the then President of India V V Giri. In 1977 his photograph Difficult Ascent was chosen from 2,500 entries from 15 Asian countries for an award in the Asia Pacific Cultural Center for the UNESCO (ACCU) Photo Contest in Tokyo, Japan. In 1980 *The Ilustrated Weekly of India* chose him from among the plethora of photographers in the country to inaugurate its photographic exhibition at the Prince of Wales Museum, Bombay, held to commemorate its centenary. In 1983 he was one among 10 eminent photographers of the world to receive the India International Photographic Council's highest honour, the Honorary Fellowship, for his outstanding contribution and selfless service to various branches of photography.

He was a master artist who never aspired for fame, yet he touched many lives, both professionally and personally. Through this exposure he became well-known in India and abroad, highly respected by his peers and the source of inspiration for a new generation of photographers. Young or old, all were his friends. Those who were lucky to have shared some time with him will always remember his vital and dynamic personality. Full of life and humour, he could entertain his friends with poetry, jokes, magic and card tricks and at the same time philosophise on life. Quite often he used to joke, "Bury my camera with me—I would need it to take pictures of angels up there."

He was one of those few great photographers who had an open mind; he had neither aversion nor fascination for any particular subject to the detriment of another. It was thus natural that his range of subjects was unlimited. Because he brought out the unique angles of all his subjects, his photographs have a contemporary quality even from today's perspective.

The bulk of his published work consists of remarkable images of day-to-day life around the country, which bring out the beauty, harmony and dignity of life and human emotions. This includes one of the most common and fascinating yet difficult subjects for photographers—children.

He was also enthusiastic about taking portraits of different people—men and women, young and old, representing different communities, religions and walks of life. A deep study of the portraits will reveal how lighting, composition, background and angle played an important role in handling each face uniquely. They are full of life, as if the sitters are face to face with us today.

Although he developed a great passion for shikar, which he learned during his forays with the Nawabs of Palanpur, he was always more attuned to capturing wildlife on film. Once, big game hunters of Gwalior assigned him the task of making a 16 mm colour film for the Zoological Society of New York on tigers in their natural habitat in Gwalior. During shooting he had a thrilling face to face encounter with a tiger. From experience he knew enough to remain still; the tiger and A L Syed stood staring at each other for a moment before the tiger roared, turned its tail and fled.

Because he studied the behaviour and unusual aspects of both domestic and wild animals, he was able to bring out their grace and charm in his pictures, often in unusual and appropriate settings. Whether a common pigeon, a goat peering out of a doorway or a wild leopard dragging its kill, he treated all with a creative touch.

He was fondly called 'The Old War Camel', for he is the only one in the country if not in the world to have captured this animal so extensively through the lens. His pictures of camels in the vast and silent desert, amid the beautiful curves and changing patterns of sand dunes and the haunting effect of changing light and sky, are like a personal interpretation of time and space.

When he shifted to Bombay it was but natural that a photographer of his eminence and fame would soon be enfolded into cinema. He made memorable stills for many films, notably *Mughal-E-Azam* and other productions of K Asif, the moghul of the film world in the 1950s.

His genre pictures are remarkable for their great depth, excellent quality and precise detail, especially those taken in and around Bombay and Palanpur. His natural skill in art is reflected in the masterful use of light for shadows, patterns and texture.

He also became a talented pictorialist with the ability to capture the mood and atmosphere of any geographical area of the country, whether it was the desert of Rajasthan, the calm, cool valleys of Kashmir or the lush beauty of the South. In fact he was the first amongst the contemporary photographers of his period to explore Kashmir and convey its beauty through photography.

In his architectural studies of monuments, buildings and sculptures, he had a great fascination for bringing out the dimensions, textures, shapes and forms in a very dynamic way, conveying the glory, majesty and grandeur of the past. He was very particular about the light conditions, atmosphere and season. Unlike the spontaneous quality of the majority of his work, here he would spend hours or even days waiting for the ideal conditions to enable him to present a new angle that would create an everlasting impression on the viewer.

The quality of his photographs is extraordinary considering the simple cameras he used throughout his career: the Senderson stand, hand-held Linhof, Autograflex, Sohoflex, Thronton Pickerd and Kodak plate cameras in various sizes. He honed his technical skills through this early experience with large format cameras, in which one plate or sheet of film produced one exposure at a time. Later he used the Rolleicord, a 12-exposure twin lens reflex camera popular among his contemporaries.

He became a perfectionist, as accuracy in focus, composition, lighting and exposure was critical. Many professional photographers prefer to leave the darkroom work to their assistants or others, but A L Syed except in much later years always insisted on doing this work himself. Whenever needed, he cropped his photographs to improve their composition, as unlike many photographers he did not believe in the need to retain the full frame.

Despite the tremendous advances in camera technology during his lifetime, he did not use gadgetry or sophisticated hi-tech equipment—exposure meter, various types of automation like built-in flash, auto loading and winding, auto focus, etc., and different lenses such as zoom and wide angle—which invaded the market and simplified photography. Even after the 35 mm became common, he preferred to use his original favourite Rolleicord and the technique that he had perfected. He did not even use the newer Rolleiflex, a more advanced version and somewhat of a status symbol.

What he produced with his simple camera is far better in spontaneity, sharpness, content and quality than what is now being produced with expensive equipment. He has proven beyond a doubt that the camera is not as important as the sincerity and devotion of the photographer.

Unlike some of his colleagues who migrated to Pakistan after Partition in 1947, Syed sahib was a true nationalist and remained in Palanpur, placing Gujarat and India on the world map. With his level of repute, he could have moved to any big metropolitan city where he would have earned a fortune, but he and his family chose to remain in Palanpur, a small, obscure town. He loved the natural surroundings with its simple folk who supported him, loved him abundantly and made him what he was. He was an ideal example of simple living and high thinking.

His dedication and accomplishments in photography were so inspiring that the next generation of the Syed family also embarked on careers in this field. The three talented sons of K L Syed—Akhtar K Syed, Asad K Syed and Shabbir K Syed—known as the 'Syed brothers', became the pride of Gujarat during their 30-year career. A L Syed's son, Azmat A Syed, is also currently running a studio in Palanpur.

From the age of 15, although success came easily to him, he never rested on his laurels. Probably no other Indian photographer has produced such marvellous works consistently and for such a long period of time. Many of his contemporaries ceased working 30 to 40 years ago, but his fingers continued to press the shutter and always at the right moment. Even after he was afflicted by the dreaded Parkinson's disease at the age of 60, he continued to work tirelessly. Although his lean frail hands shook uncontrollably trying to grip even the lightest objects, when it came to holding a camera, surprisingly, his hands would remain rock steady enabling him to continue to produce stunning pictures of lasting value.

However, in the late eighties his health began to deteriorate rapidly and he was unable to continue working. Having devoted his entire life to photography, he mourned the closure of that chapter in his life. But he also lamented the quickly deteriorating standards of photography in the country, as contemporary photographers and photojournalists became consumed with producing for the international market images of poverty and the human being in misery. For a man who had maintained a very high level of integrity and preserved the dignity of the human spirit in all aspects of his work, this was difficult to both witness and accept. Further encouraged by his guru, in 1989 he chose to renounce the world and become a fakir. It was so simple in his own words: "I have seen everything, hence I have left everything."

On 30 August 1991, the legendary A L Syed, a pioneer in the true sense and the 'eye of the century', passed away, and a golden era in Indian photography came to an end. But his wonderful deeds and creations throughout his life have immortalised him.

O P Sharma

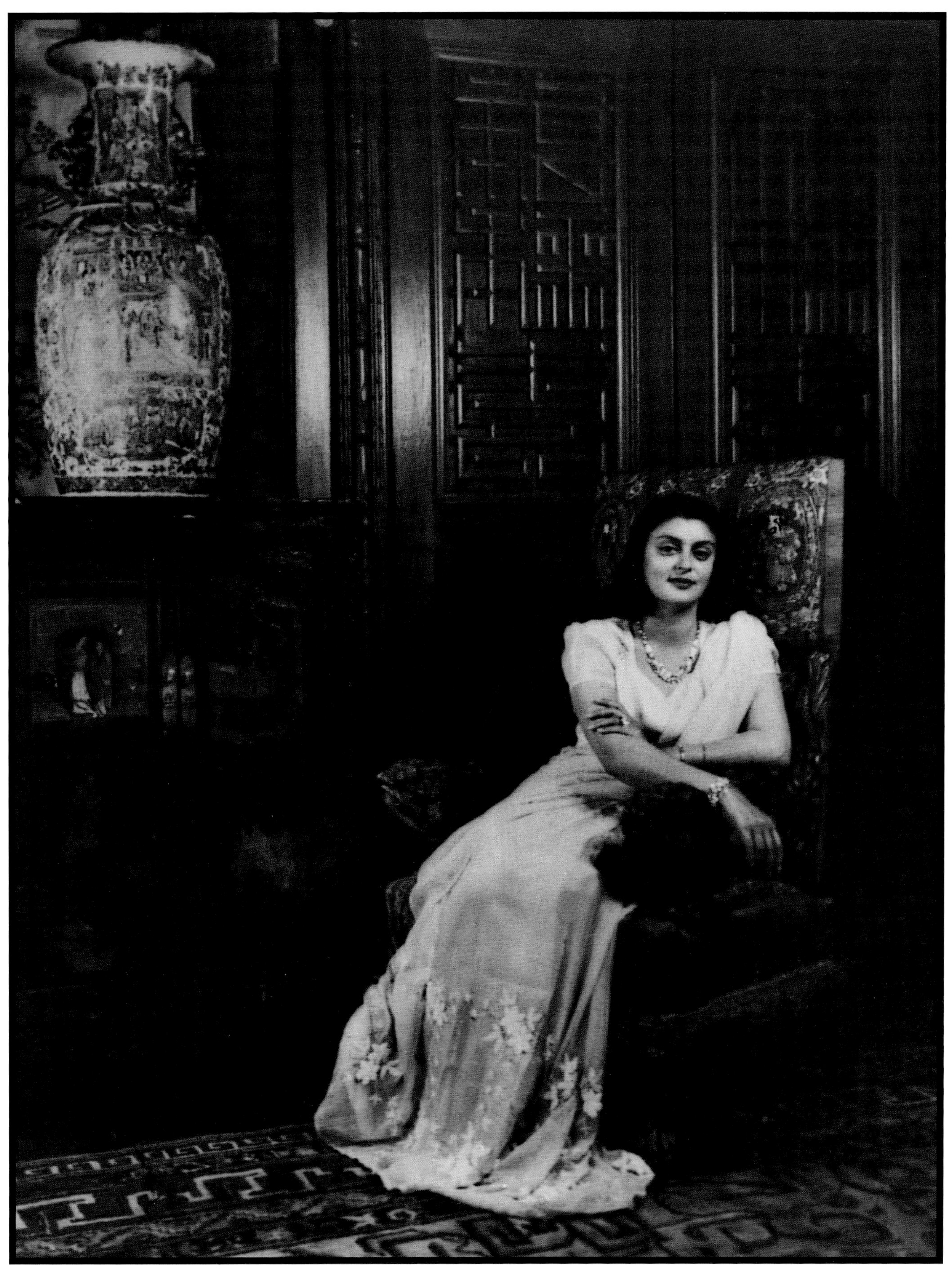

Rajmata Gayatri Devi of Jaipur

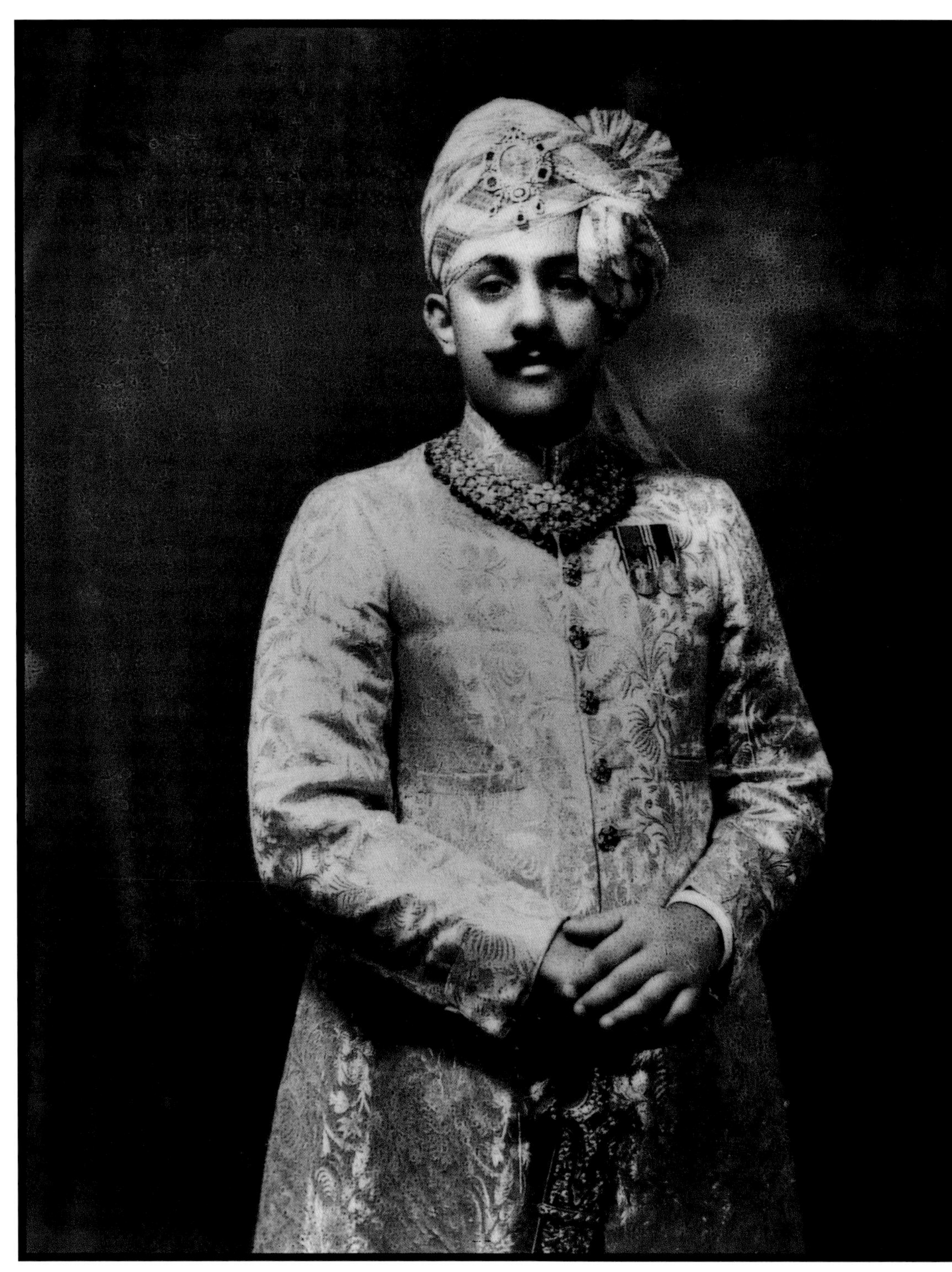

Abid Mian became my companion and friend—he also taught me photography. He was a mild, affable and witty person and it was fun having him around. We of Palanpur are proud of his achievements. I am so happy a book on his photographs is being published, as it is long overdue. It will be, I am sure, an inspiration to all young up-and-coming photographers.

Nawab Iqbal Mohamed Khan of Palanpur

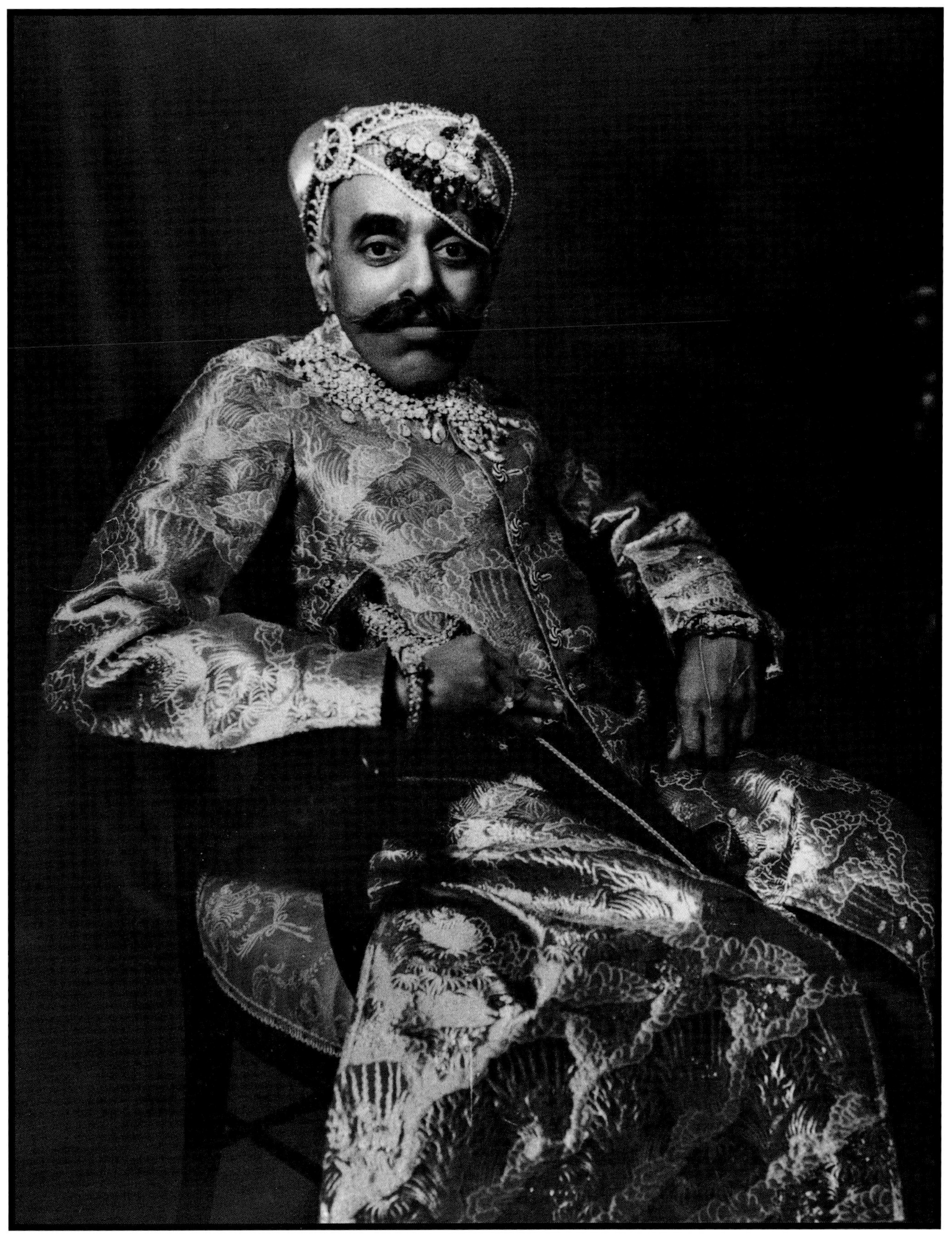

Maharana Bhupat Singhji of Udaipur

Left: Present Nawab Iqbal Mohamed Khan of Palanpur

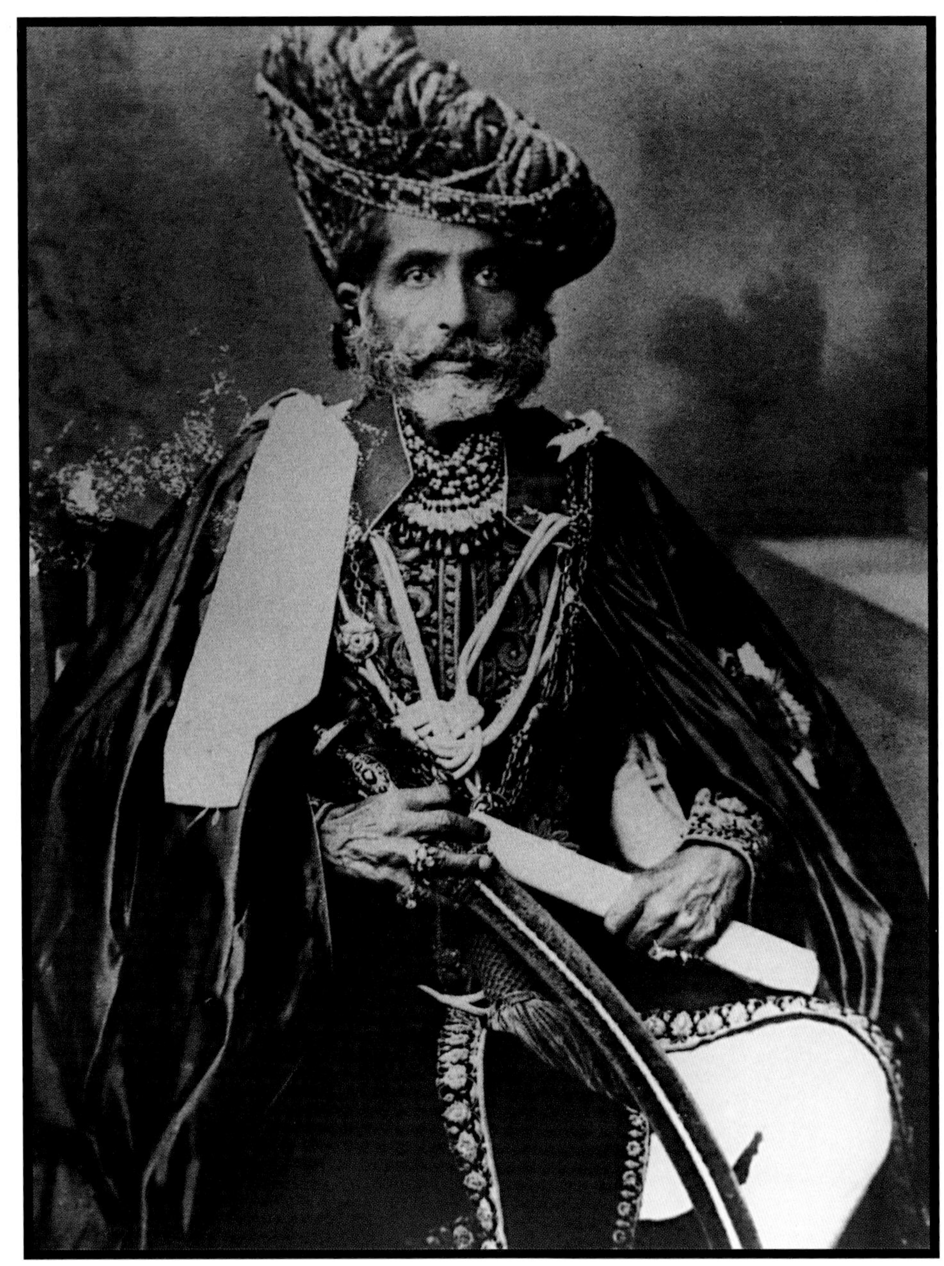

Our family and the Syed family have had a very close relationship for over five generations, as my great grandfather and my grandfather were both attached to the Nawab sahib of Palanpur as courtiers. I have photographs taken by Shri A L Syed and his son right from the time of my grandfather. I am happy that a book is being brought out on his life.

B K Gadhvi
Former Minister of State for Finance

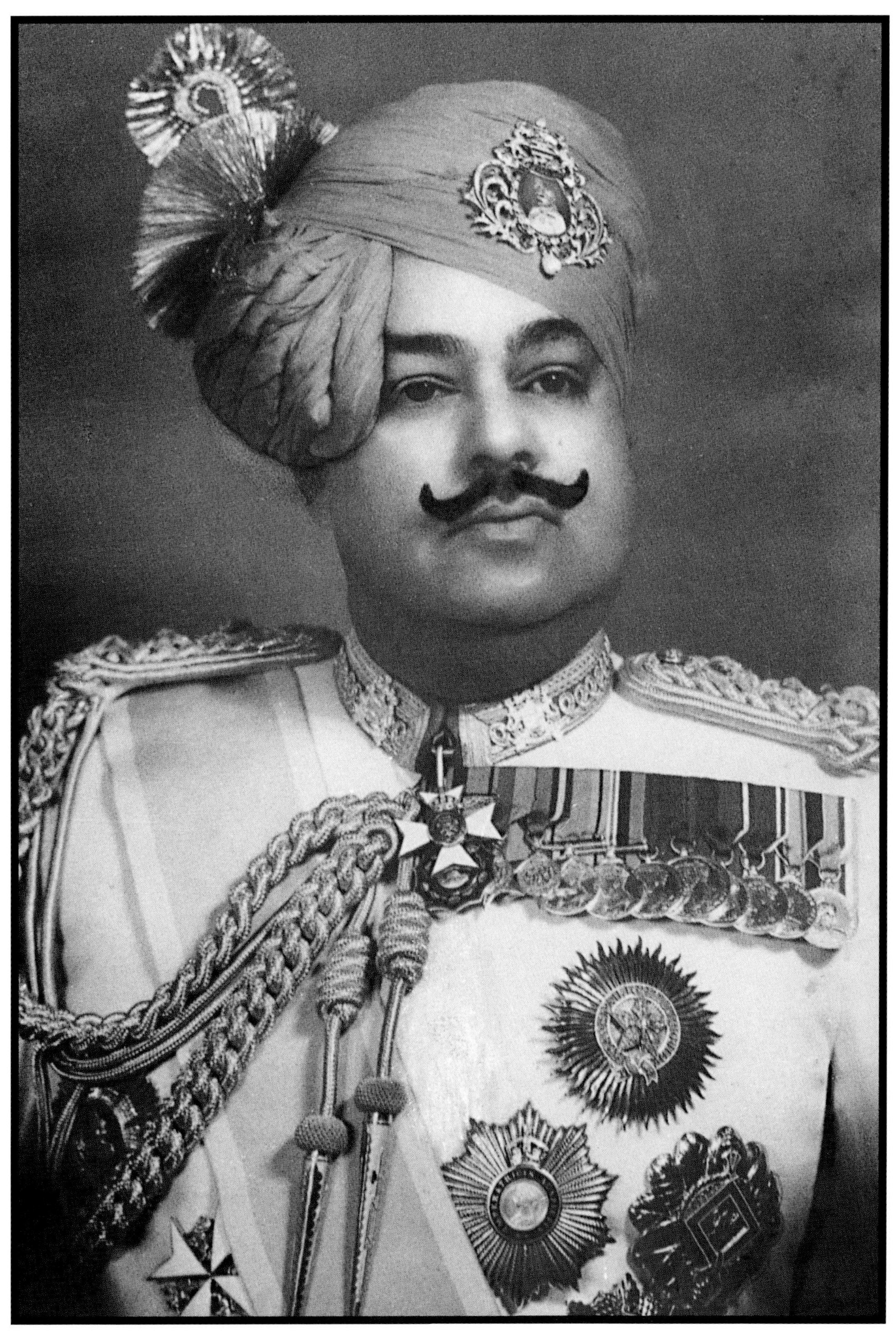

H H Shardul Singhji of Bikaner

Left: Late Nawab Sher Mohamed Khan of Palanpur

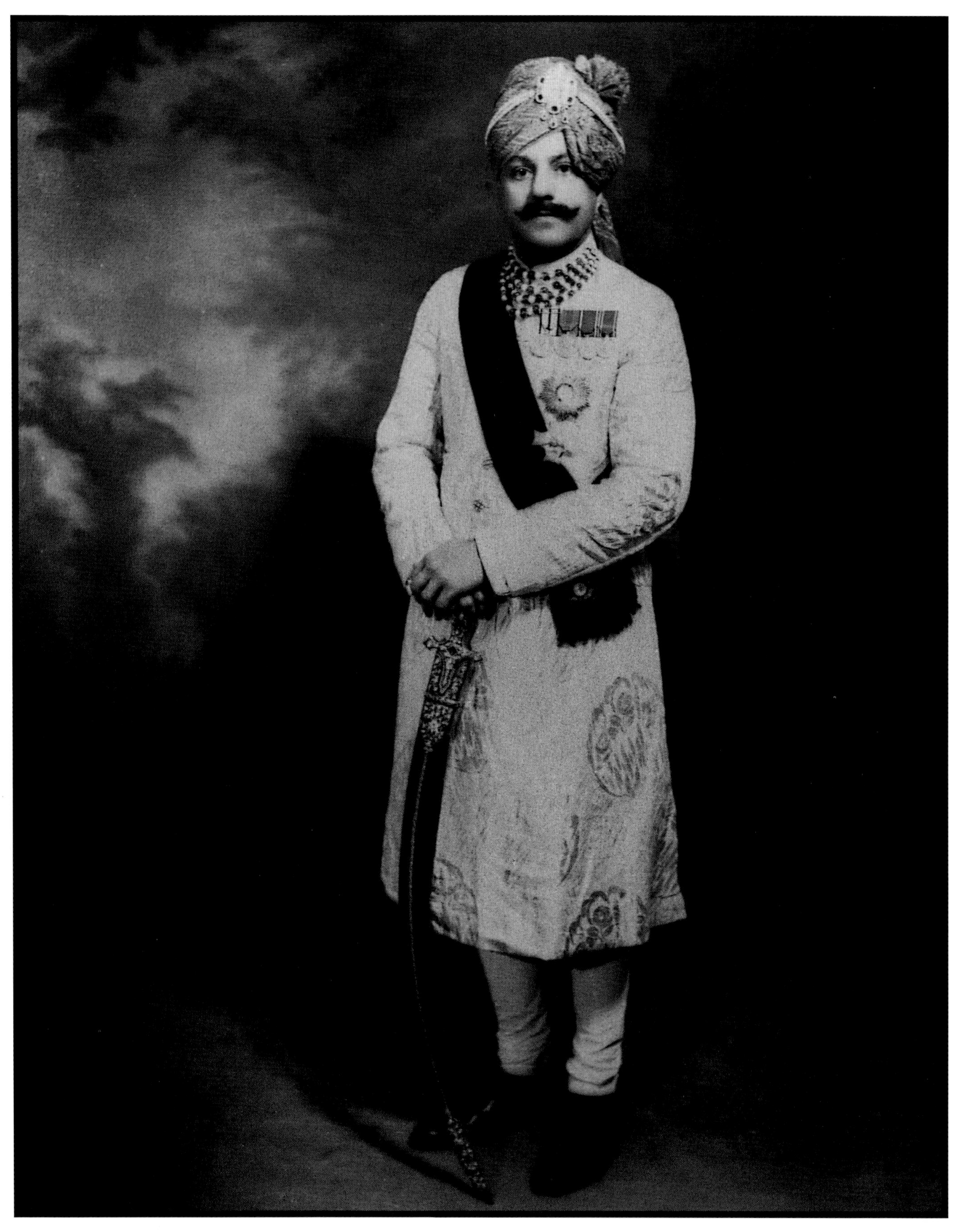

Late Nawab Tale Mohamed Khan of Palanpur

Right: Late Maharao Umed Singhji of Kotah

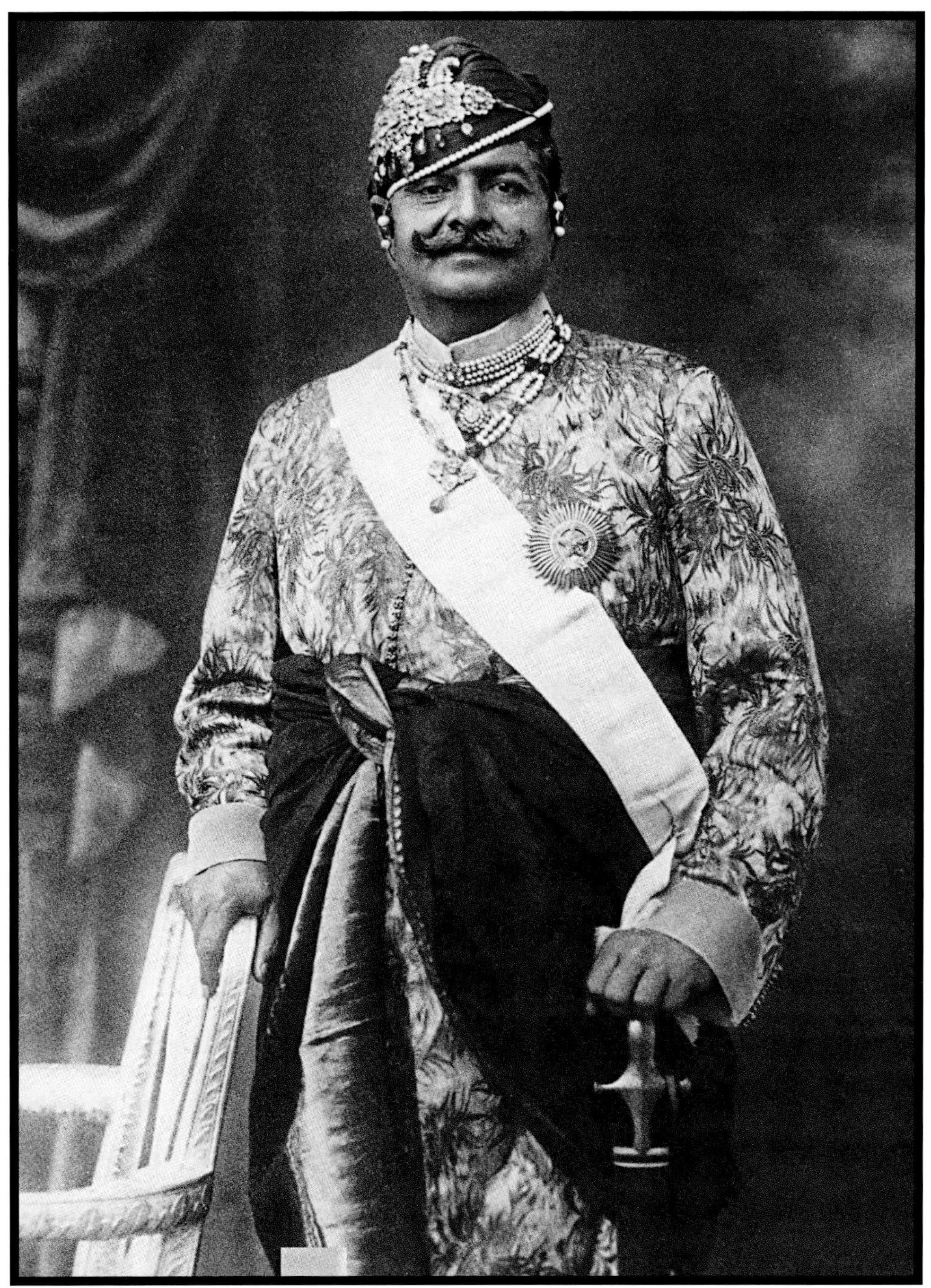

I grew up knowing the name Abid Mian. Later I met the man and got to know him. He came to cover all the important events in our family and took some of the first photographs of my children. I have a wonderful photograph that he took of my baby daughter and me when she was hardly a month old. It is a classic!

He is greatly missed, for men of his calibre and character are rarely found today.

H H Maharao Brijraj Singh of Kotah

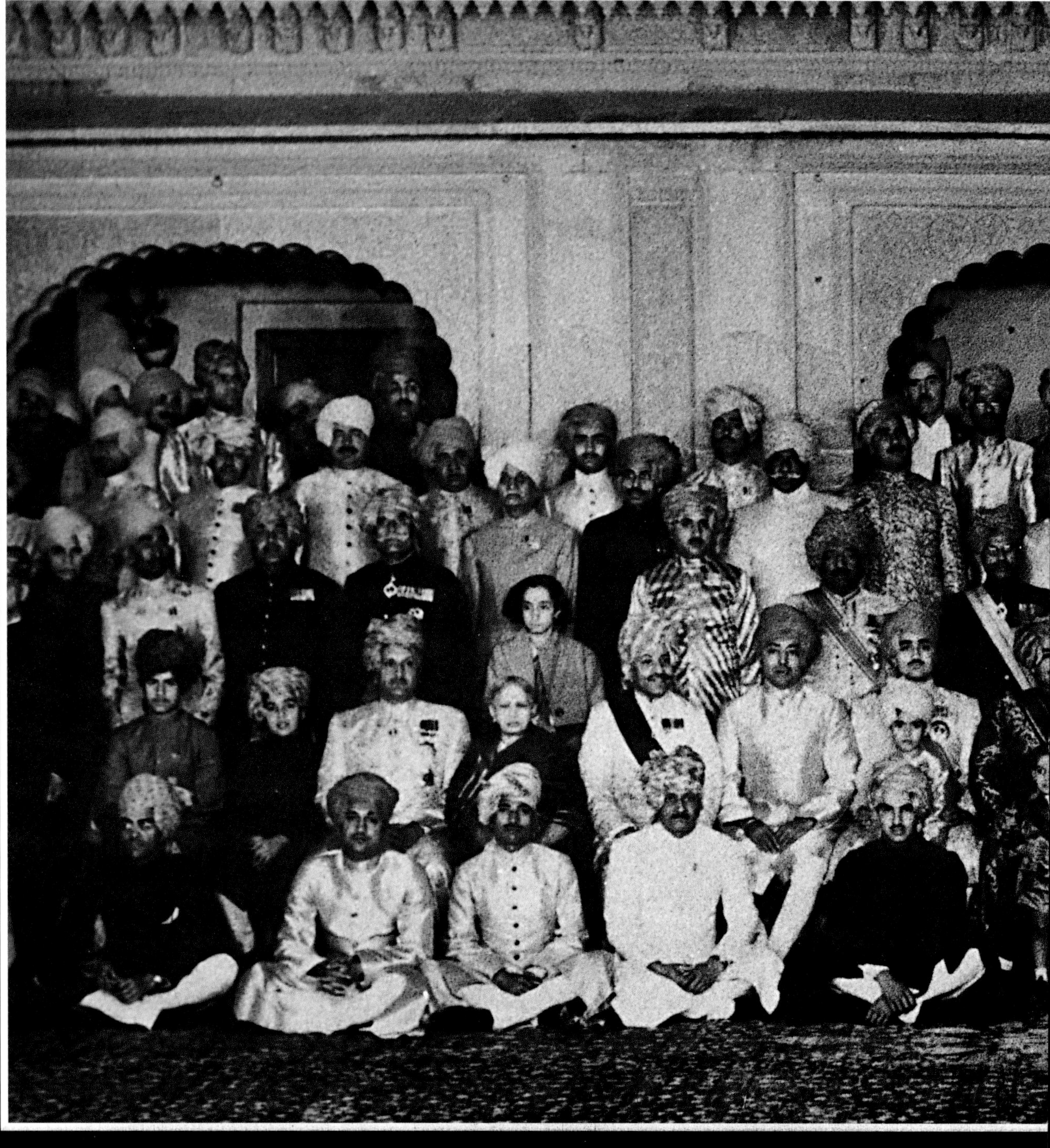

Marriage of Yuvaraj of Bikaner

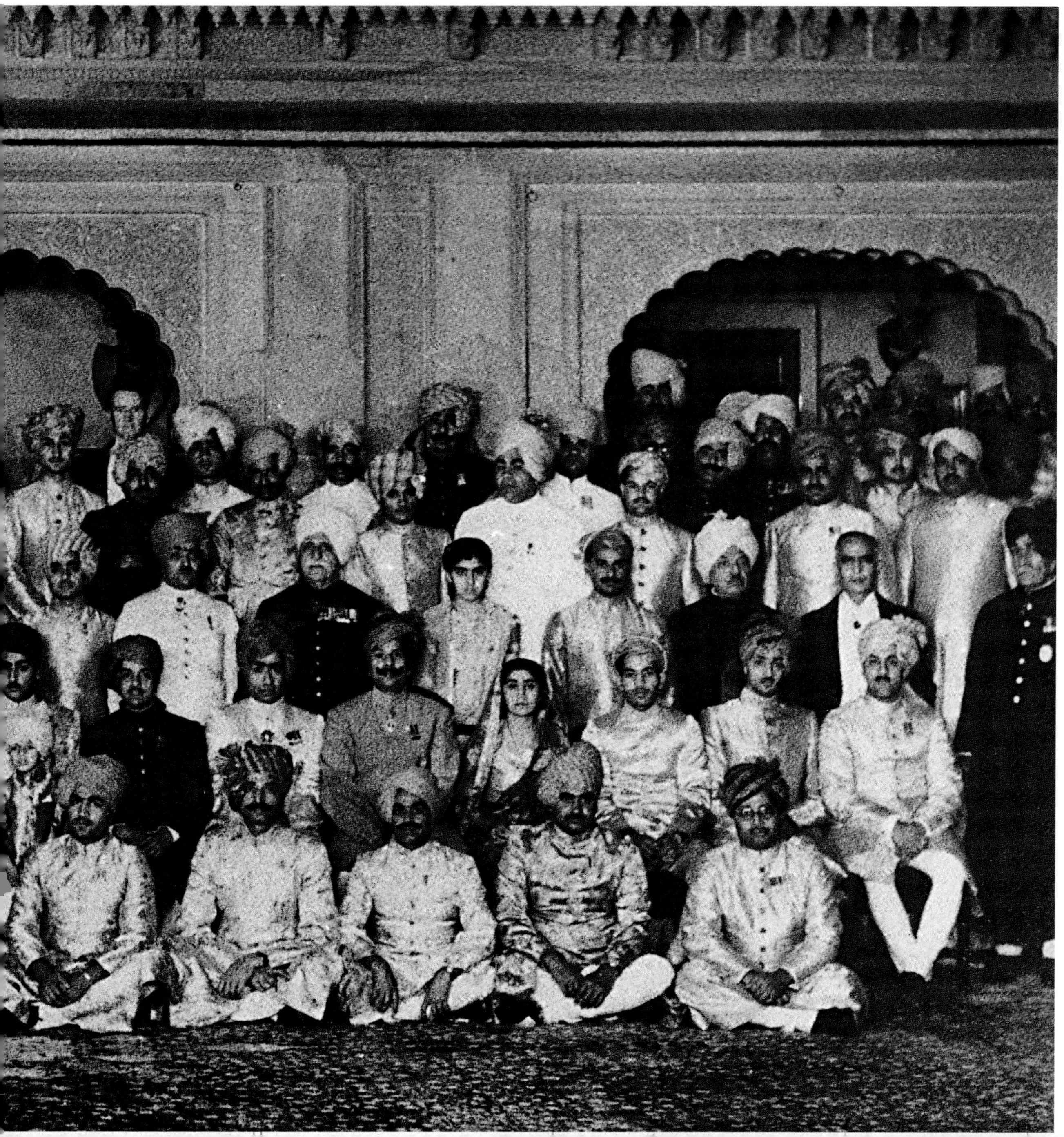

Some years ago my revered husband
Maharaja Dr. Karni Singhji Bahadur of Bikaner,
himself a keen photographer, inaugurated an
exhibition of the works of Shri A L Syed at
Jahangir Art Gallery in Mumbai, which was a
great success. A L Syed's contribution in
the development of photography in India will
always be remembered by the coming
generations of artists.

Rajmata Sushila Kumari of Bikaner

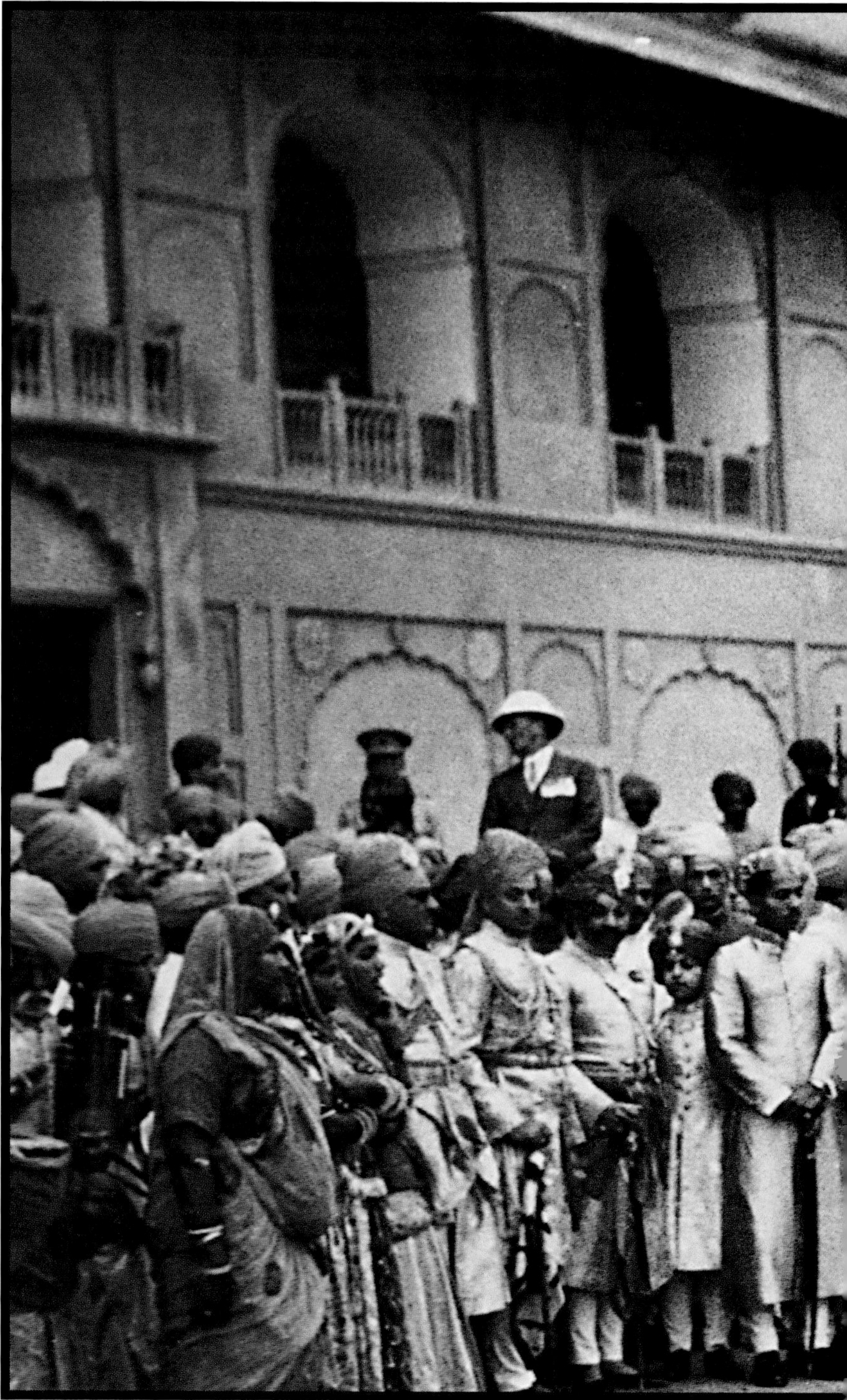

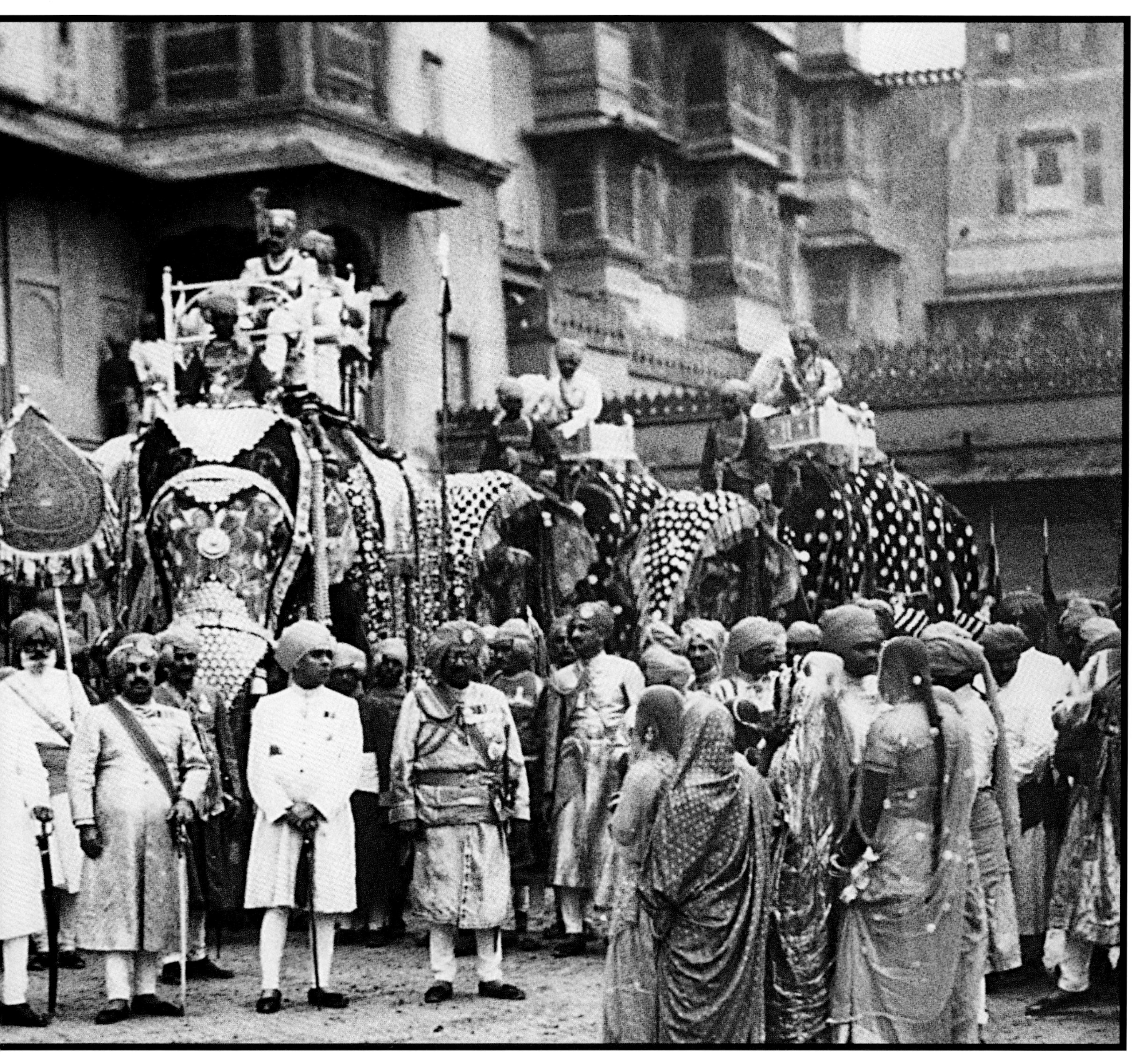

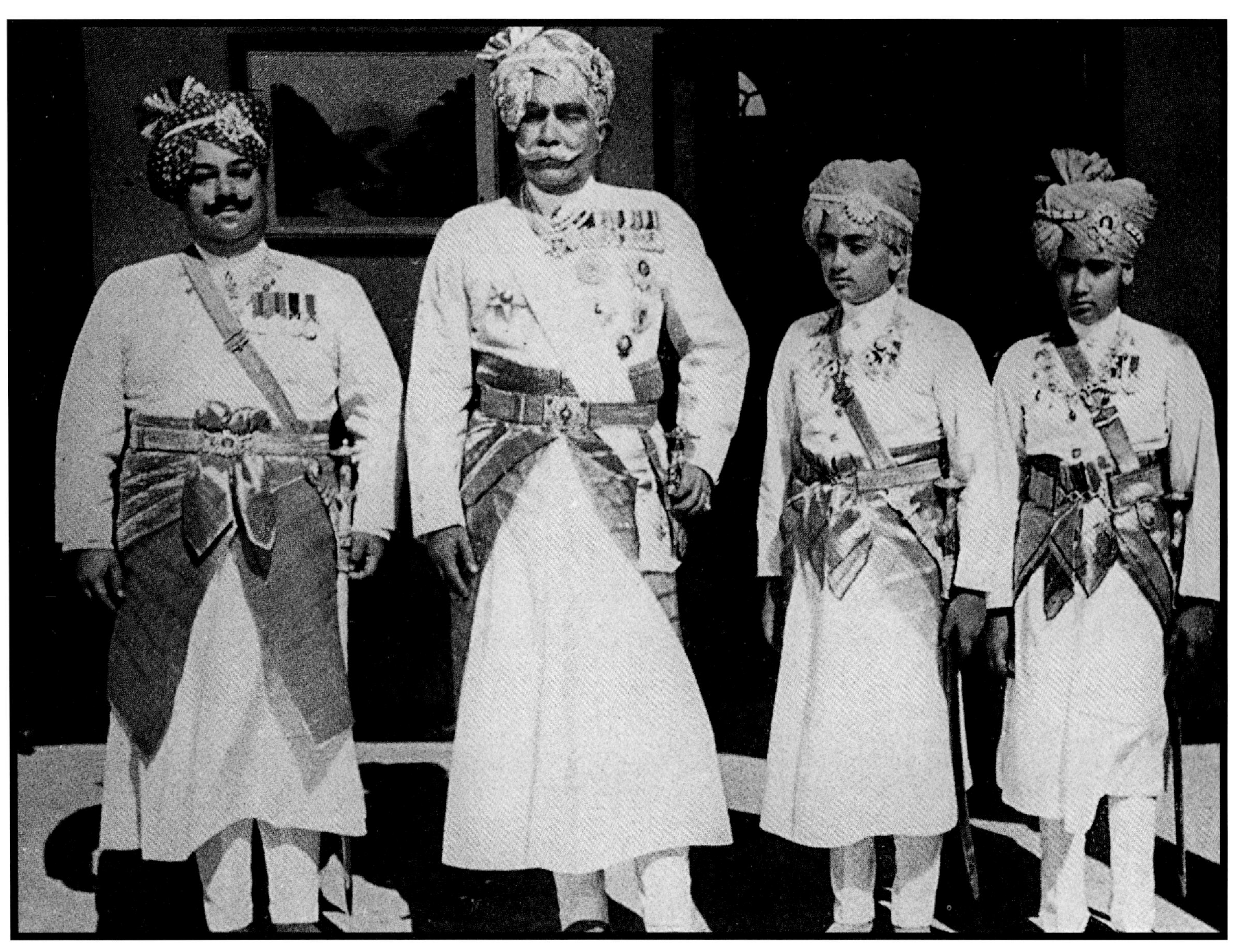

Maharaja Kumar Shardul Singhji, H H Ganga Singhji, Rajkumar Karnai
Singh and Rajkumar Amar Singh of Bikaner

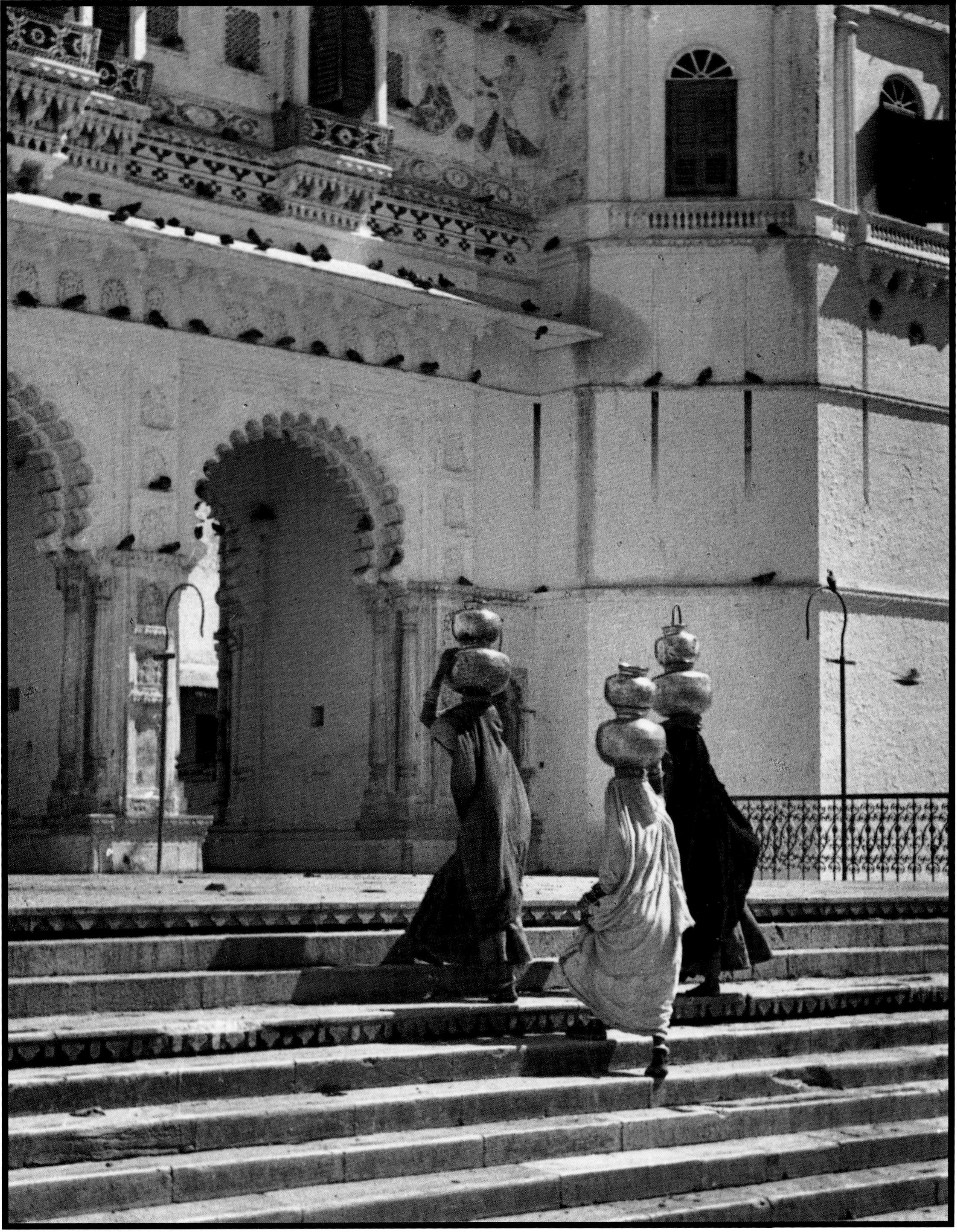

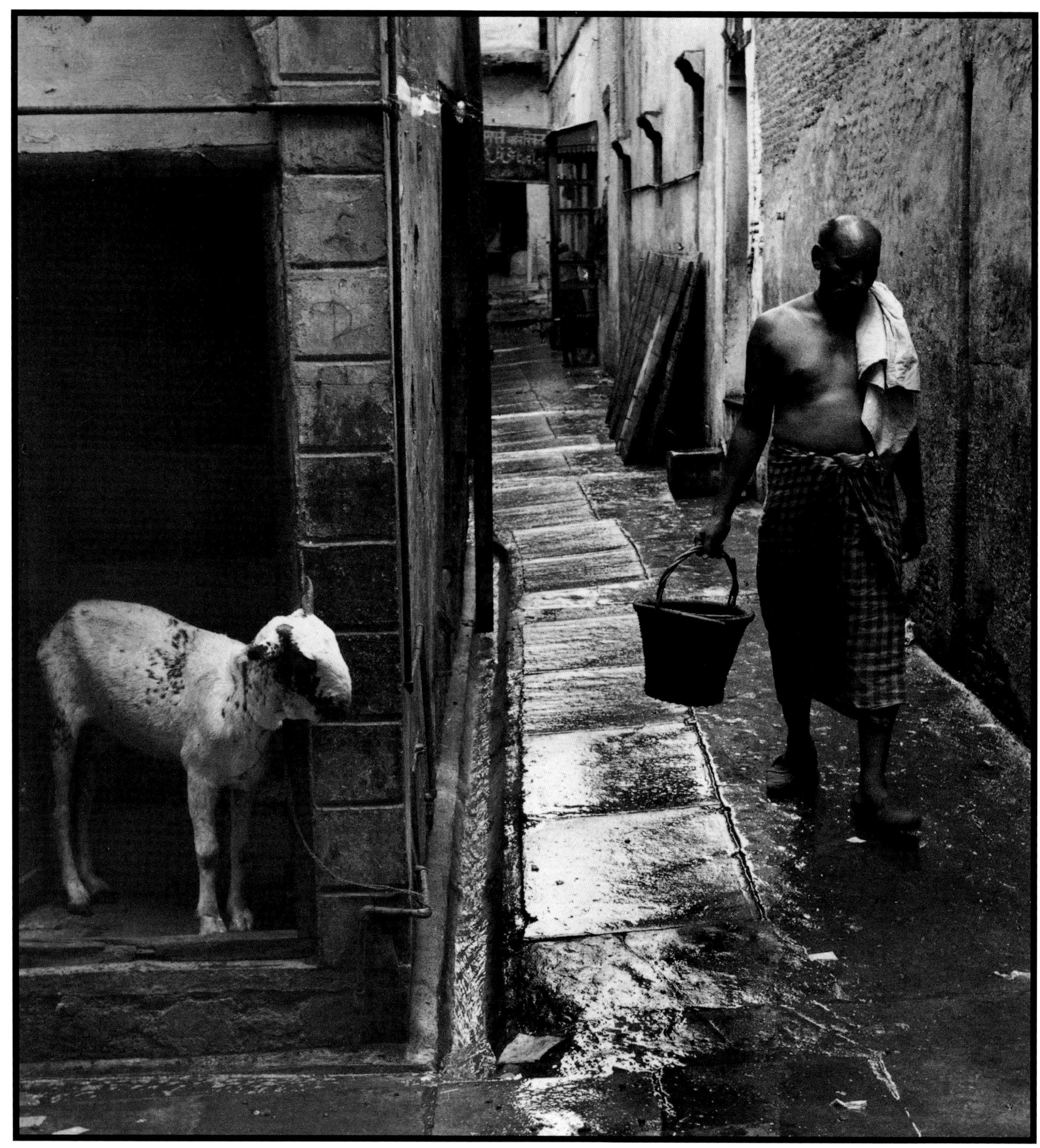

Drizzle in old Delhi

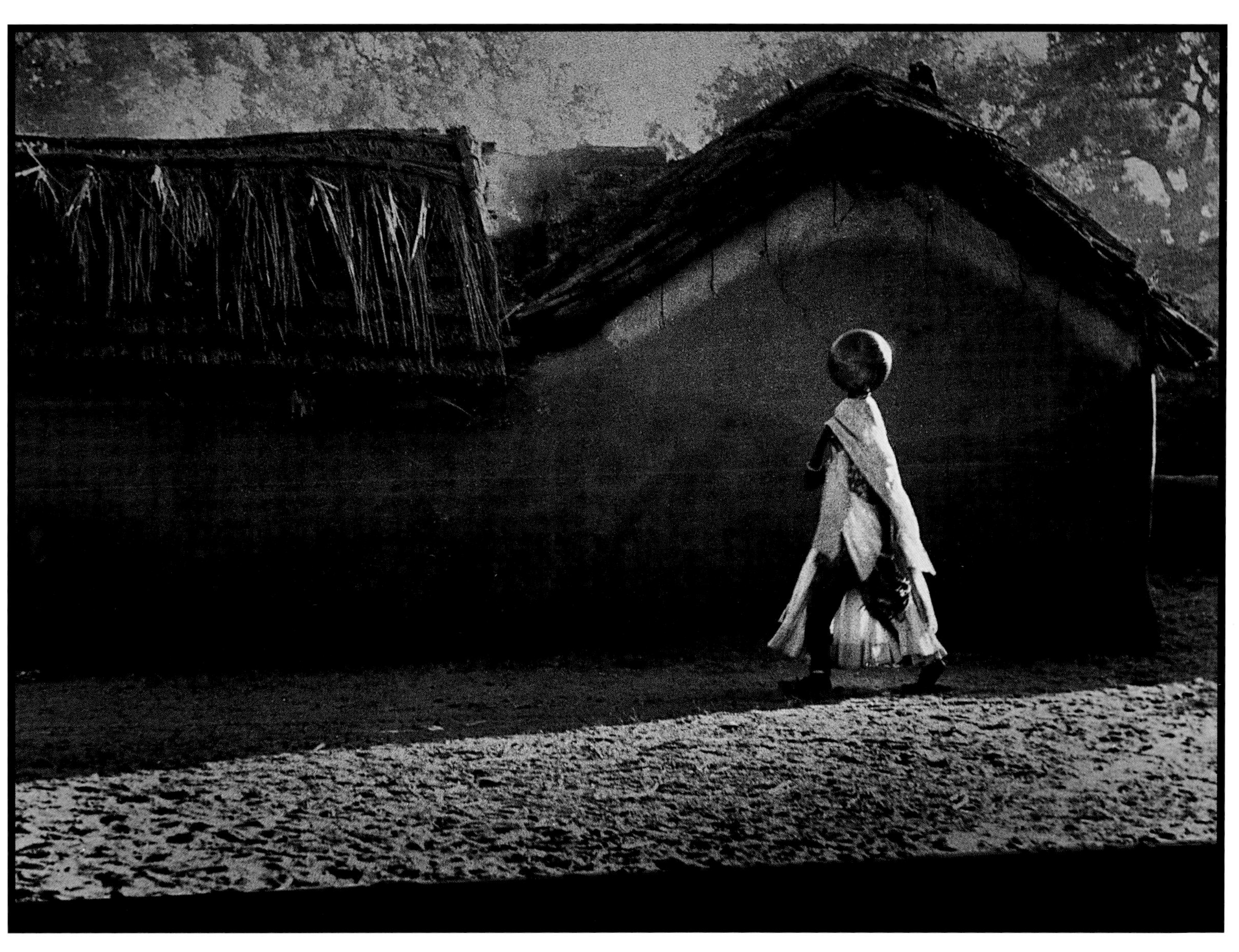

Desert morning, Rajasthan

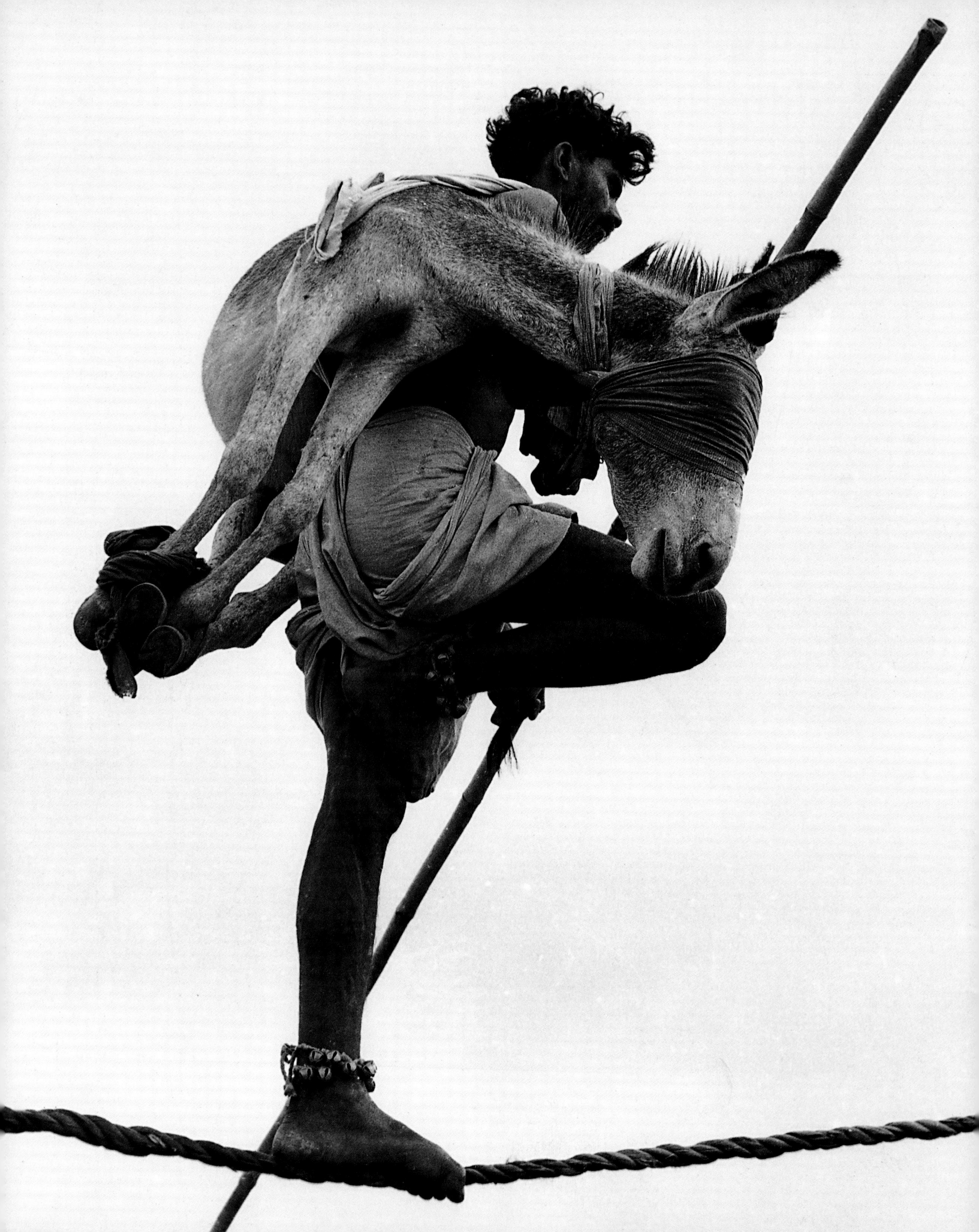

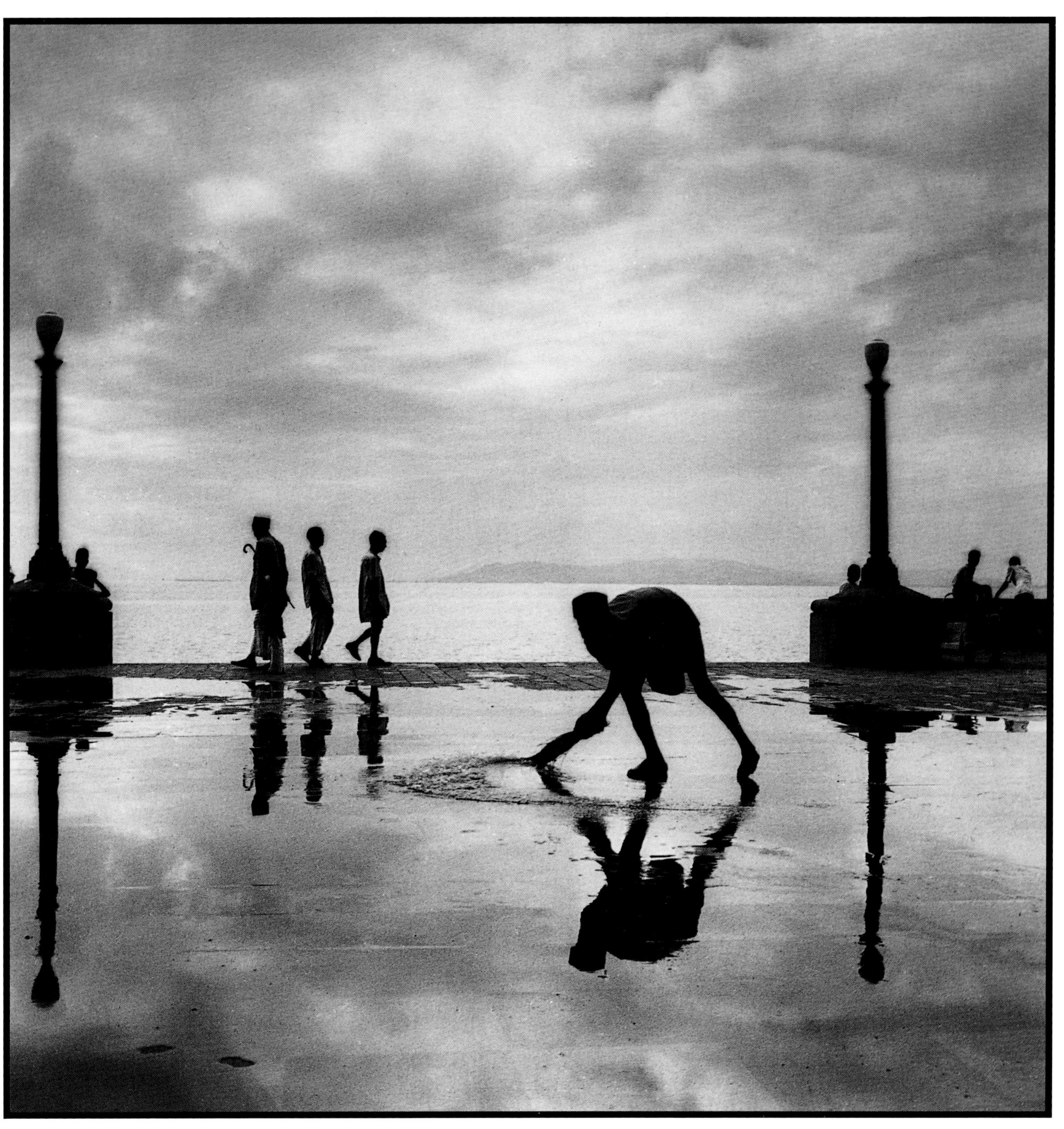

Monsoon at the Gateway of India, Bombay

Left: Risky balance, Sanali, Gujarat

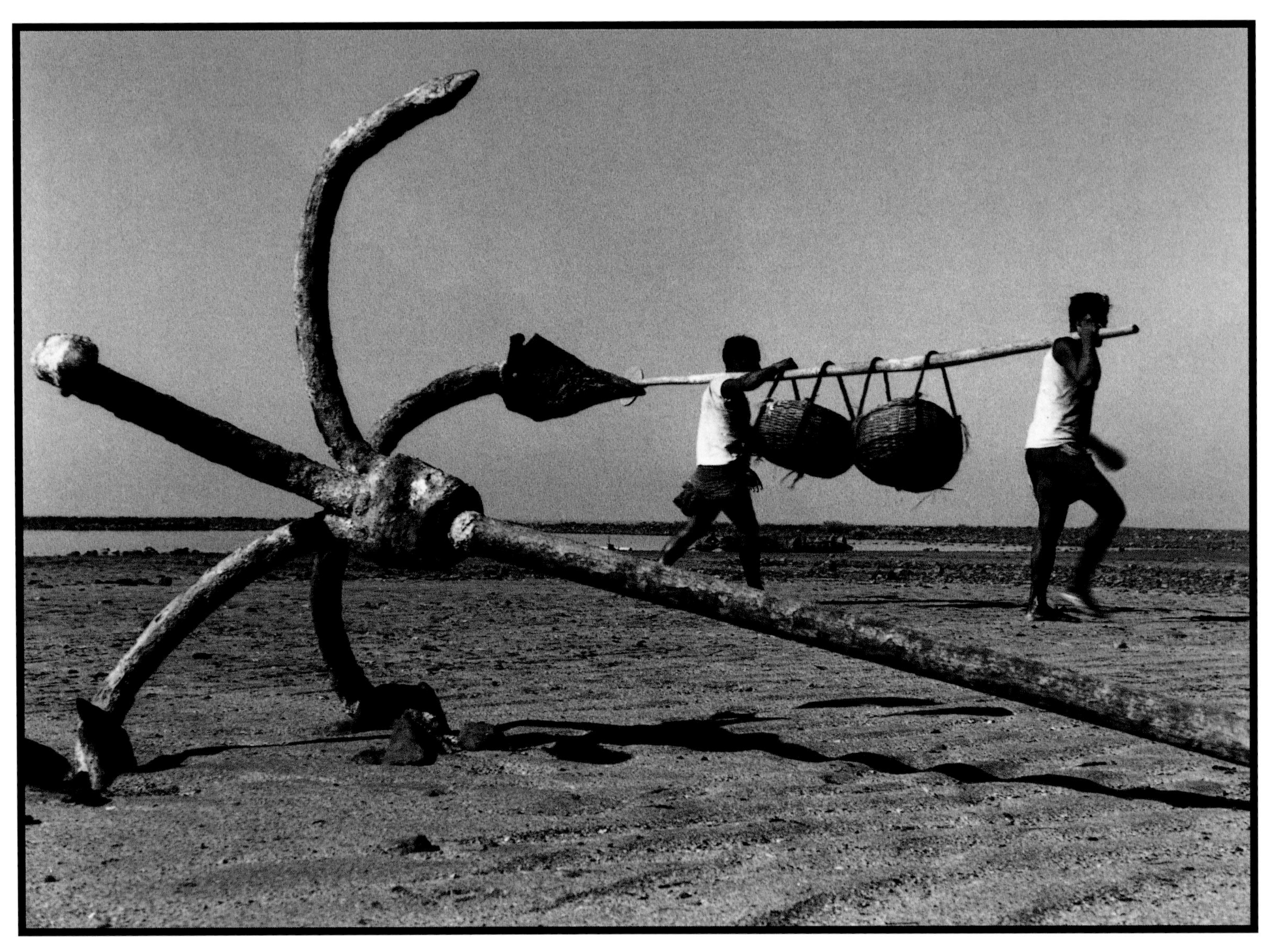

After the catch, Juhu, Bombay

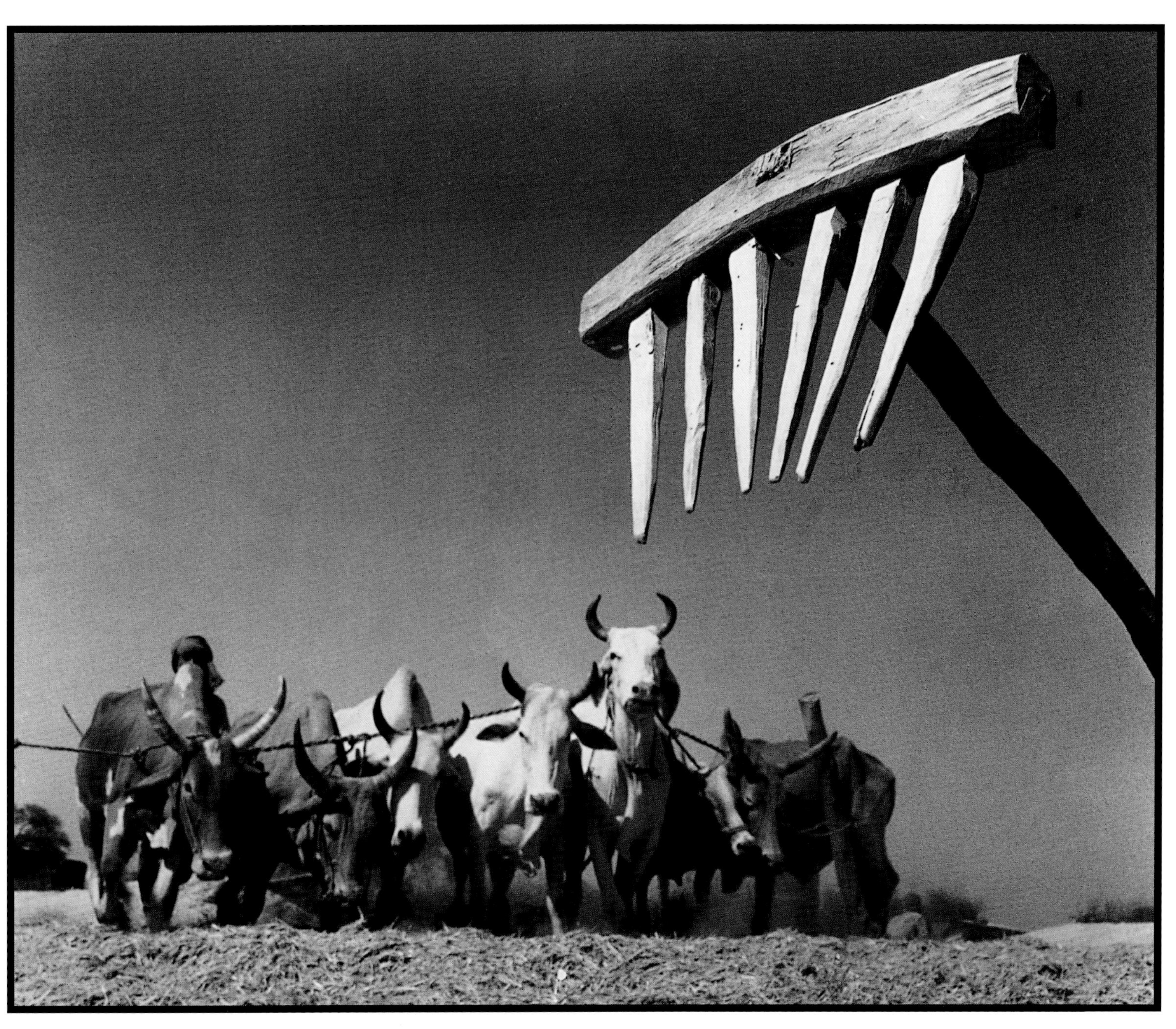

Farming in Gujarat

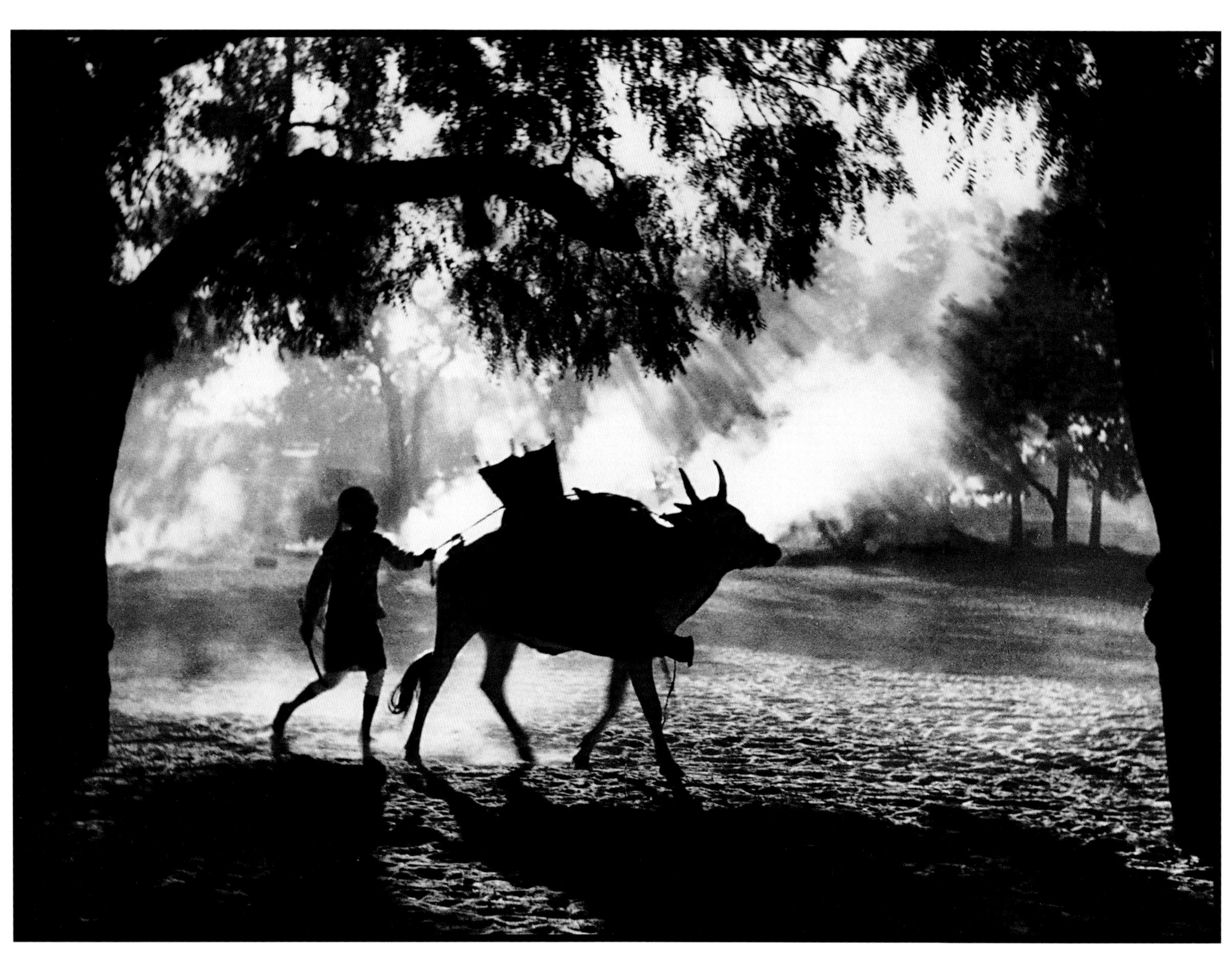

To the destination, Palanpur (Box Camera picture, 1926)

Right: Winter dawn, Palanpur

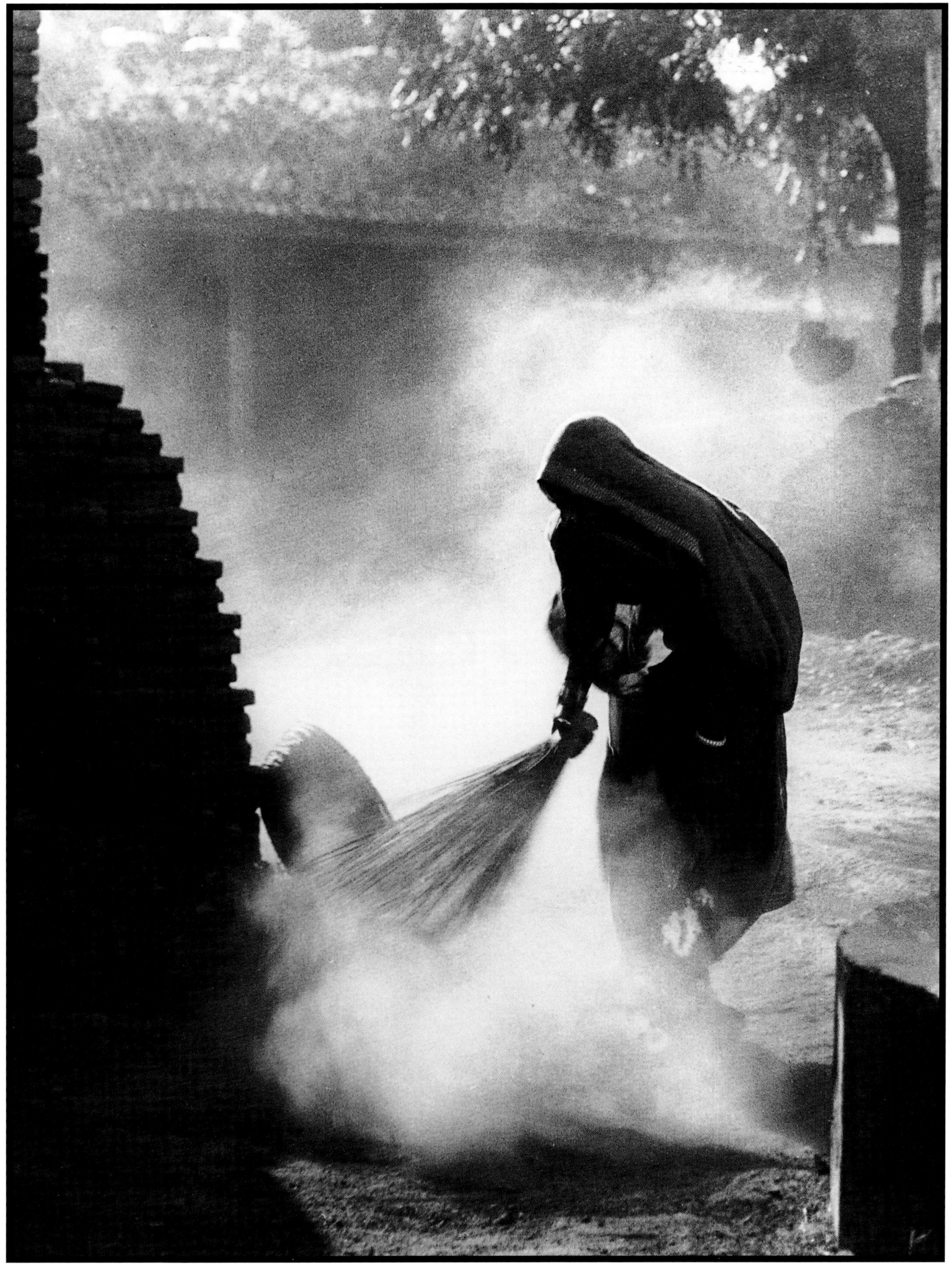

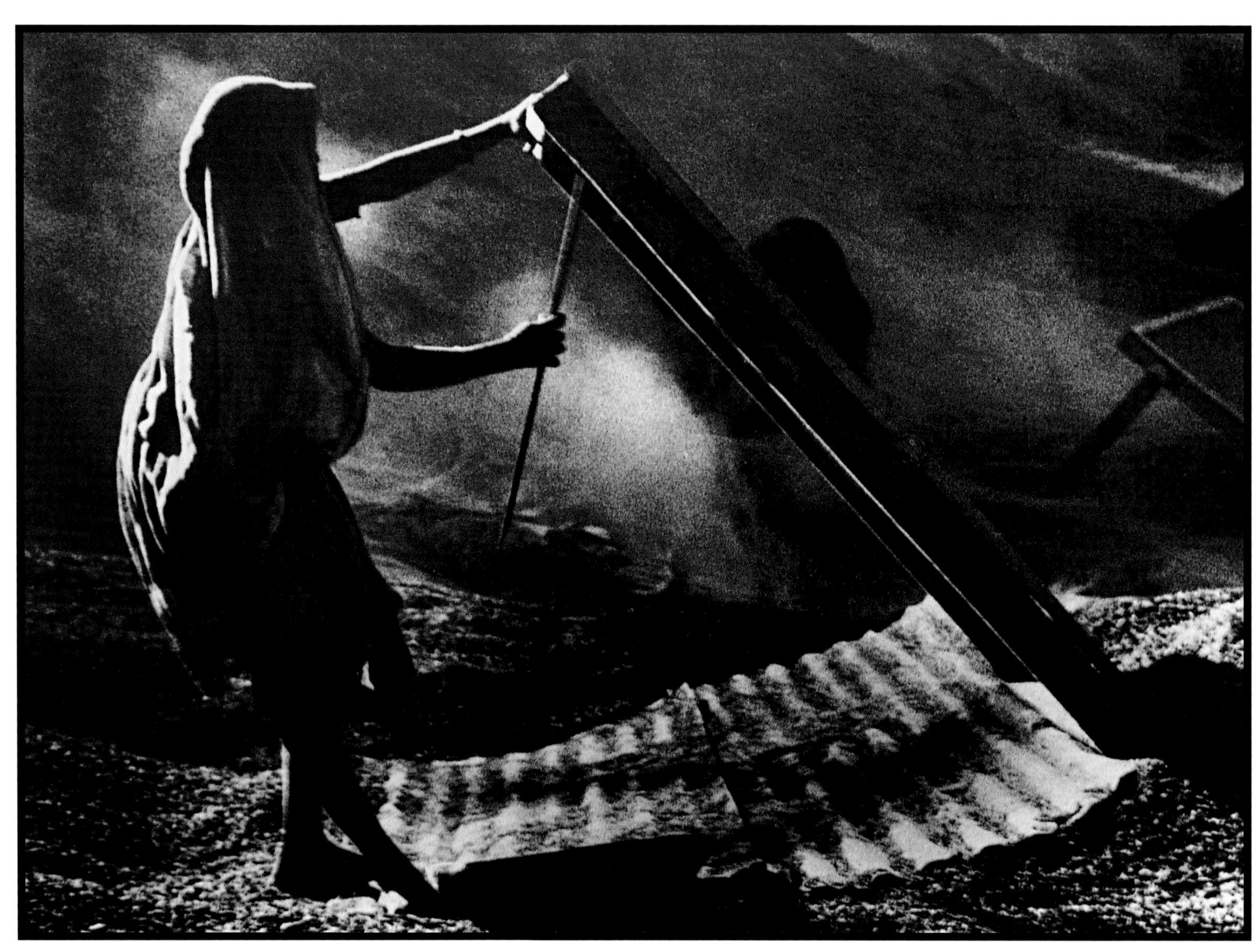

Working at dawn, Maharashtra

Right: Farmer girl, Rajasthan

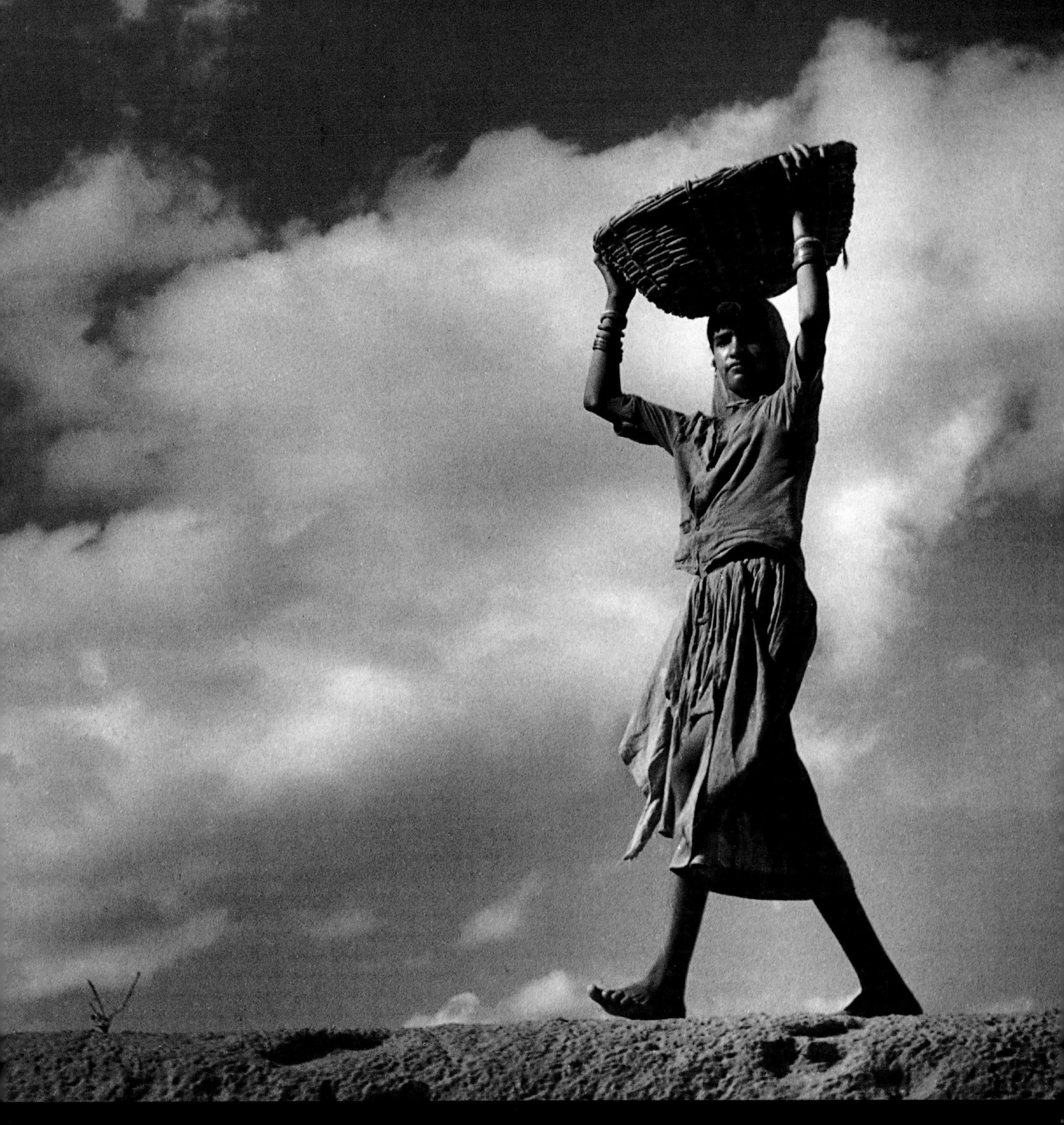

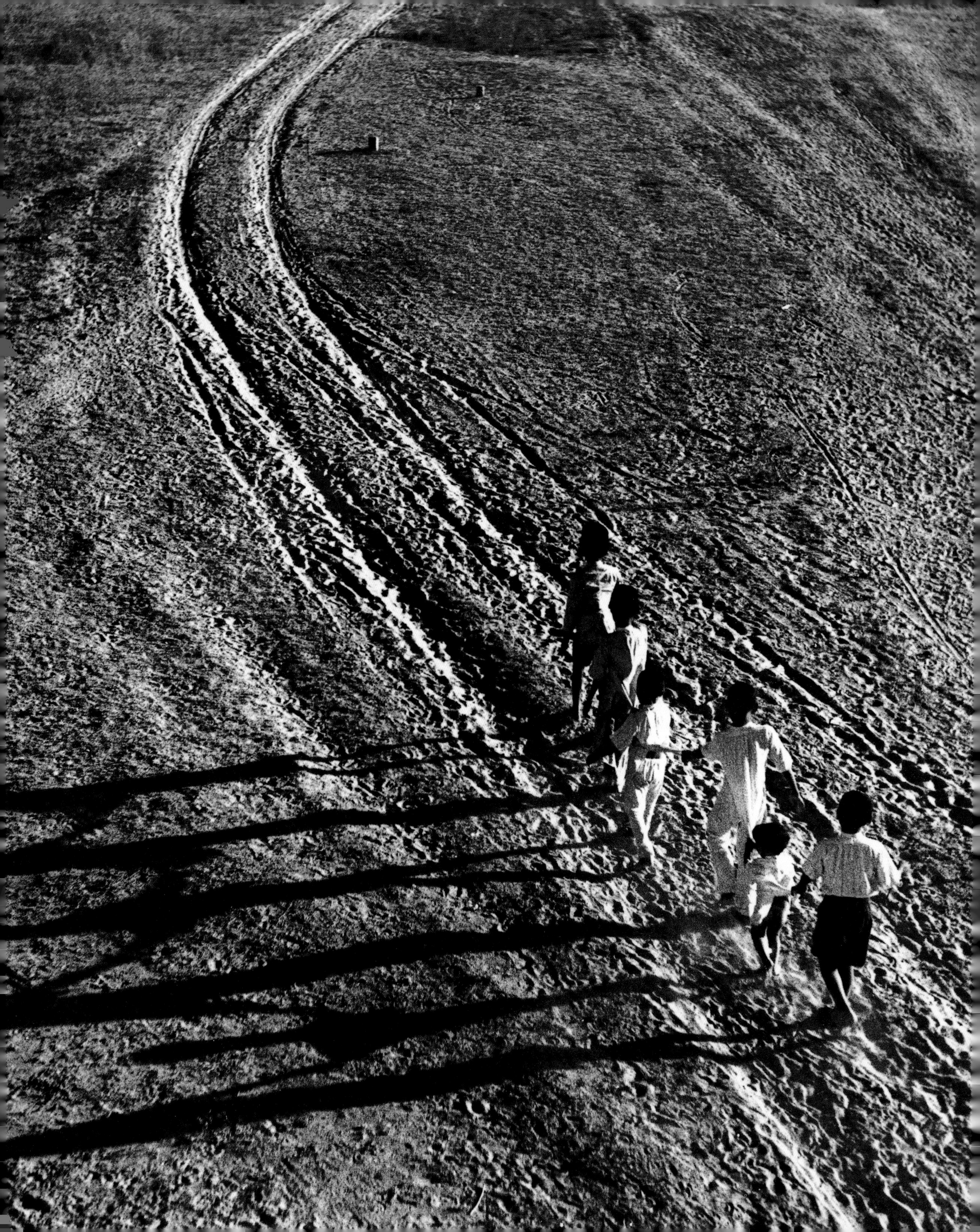

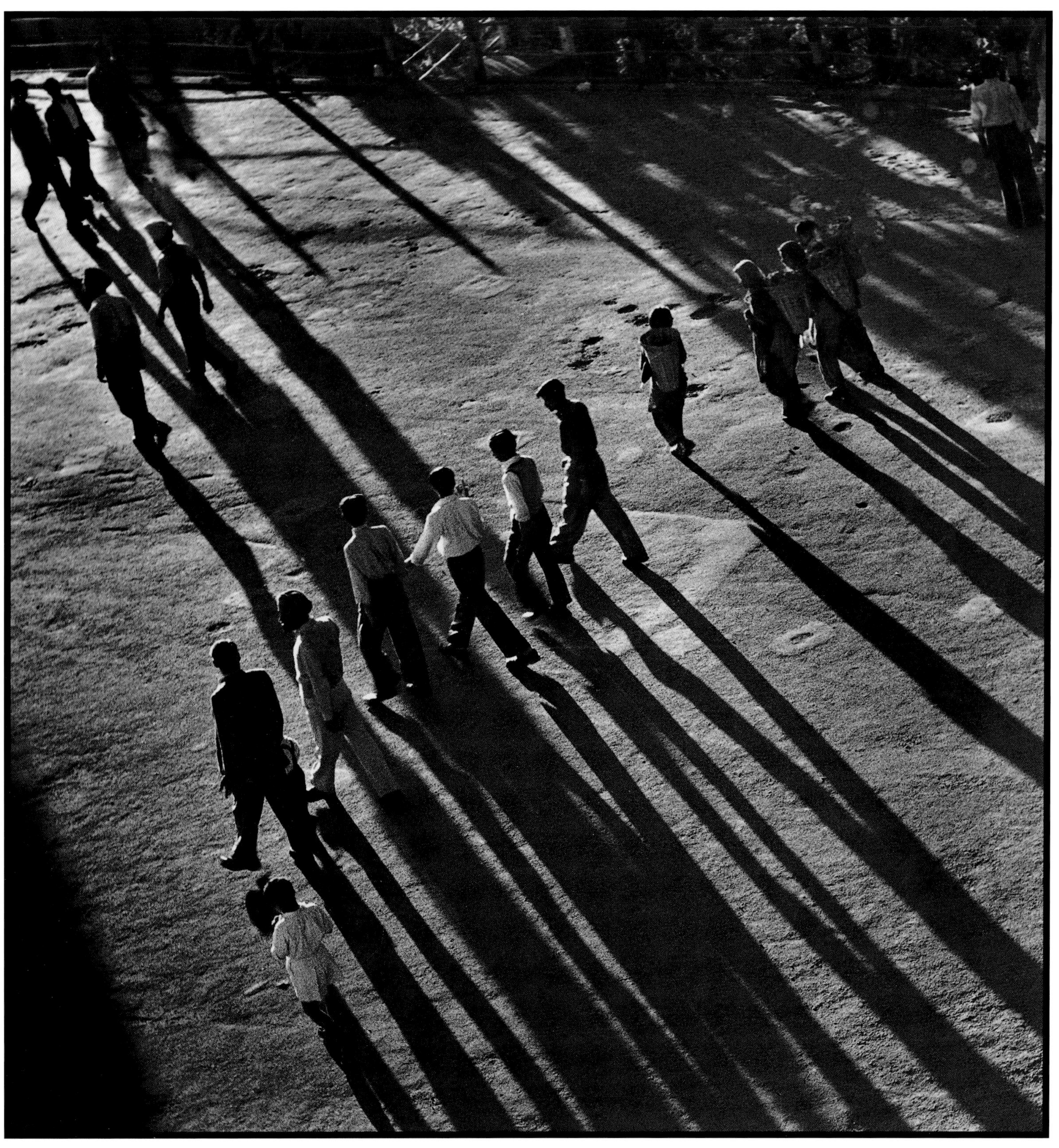

Rush hour, Shimla

Left: On the track, Palanpur

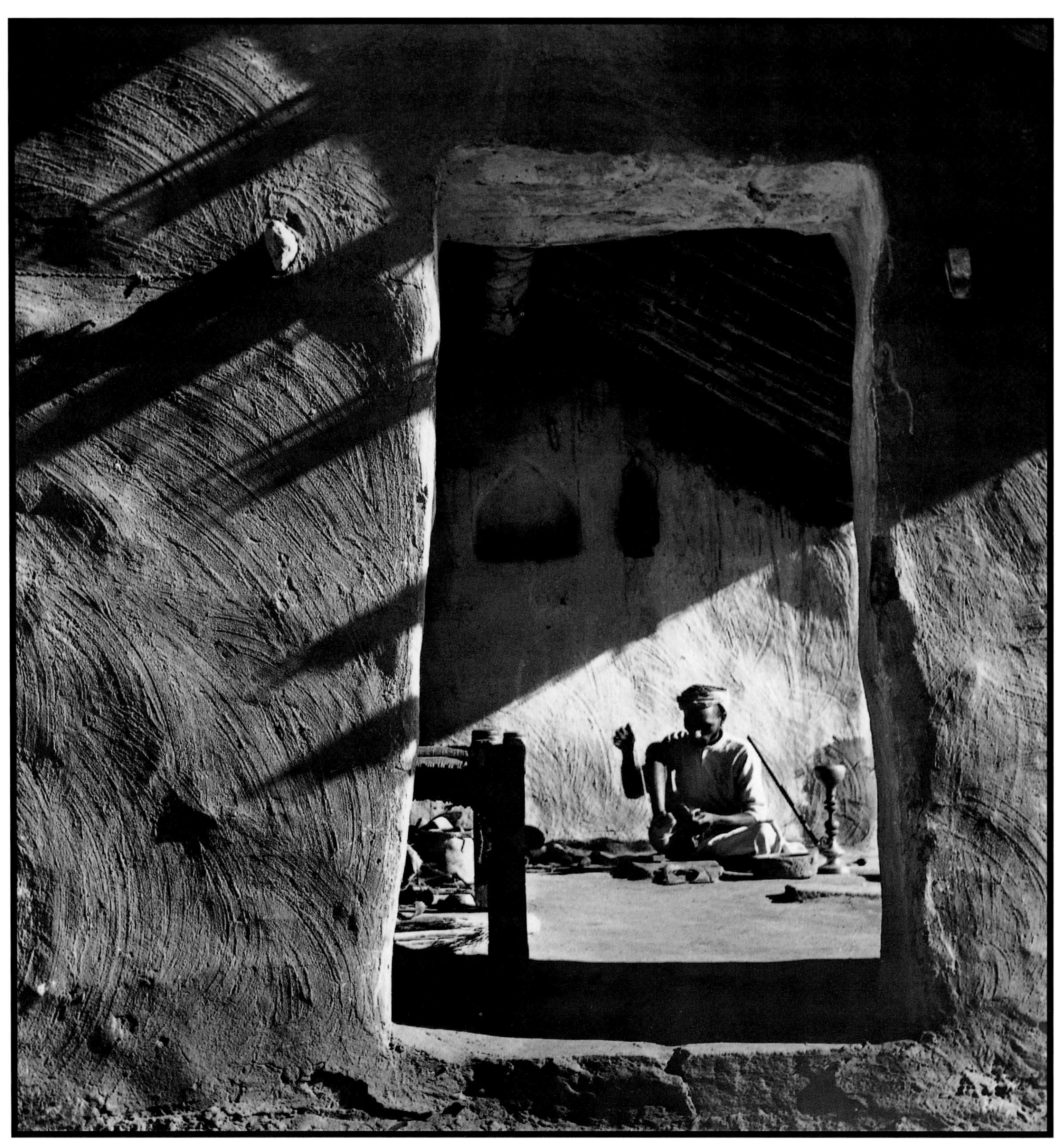

Village cobbler, Rajasthan

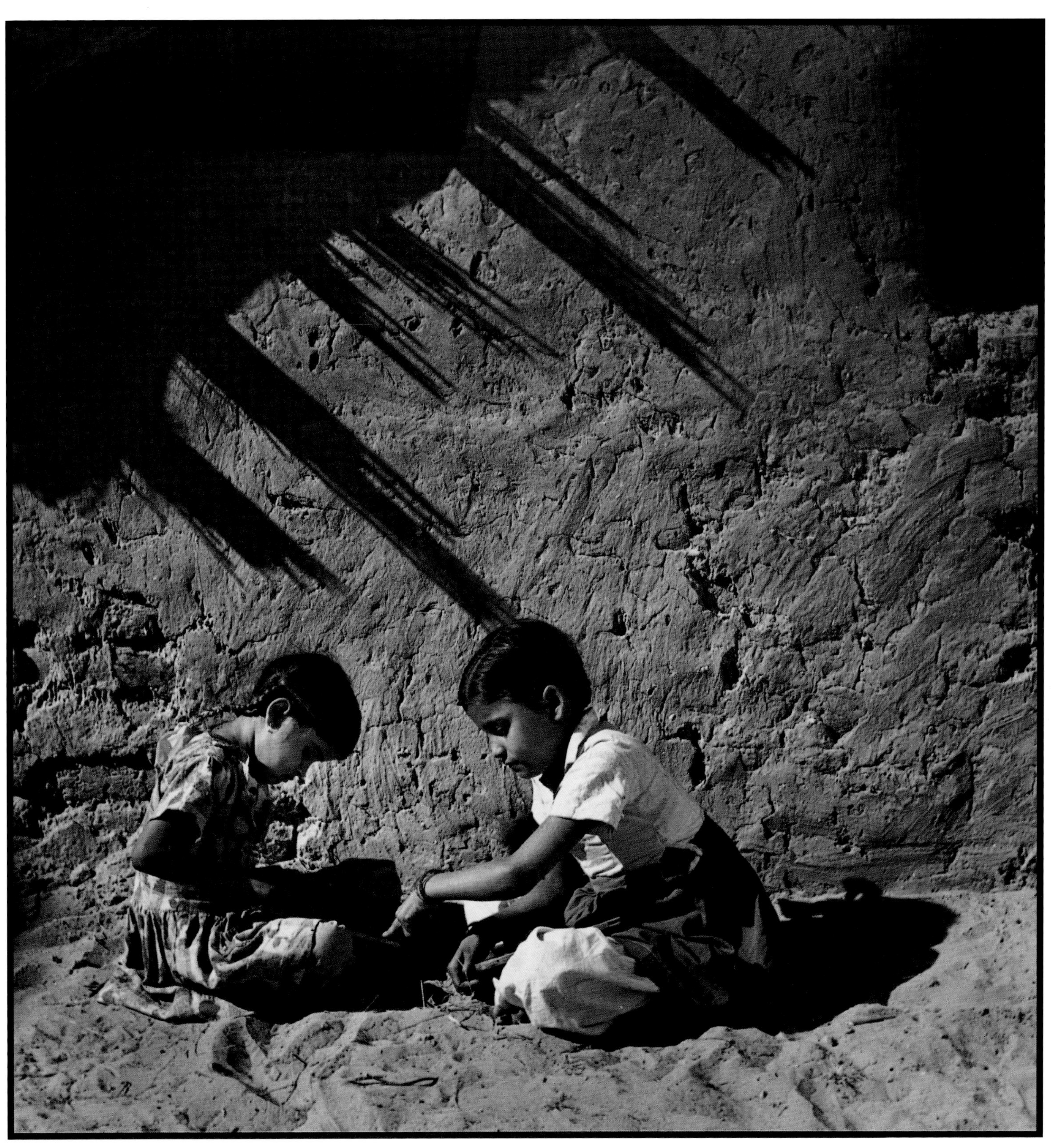

Study corner, Rajasthan

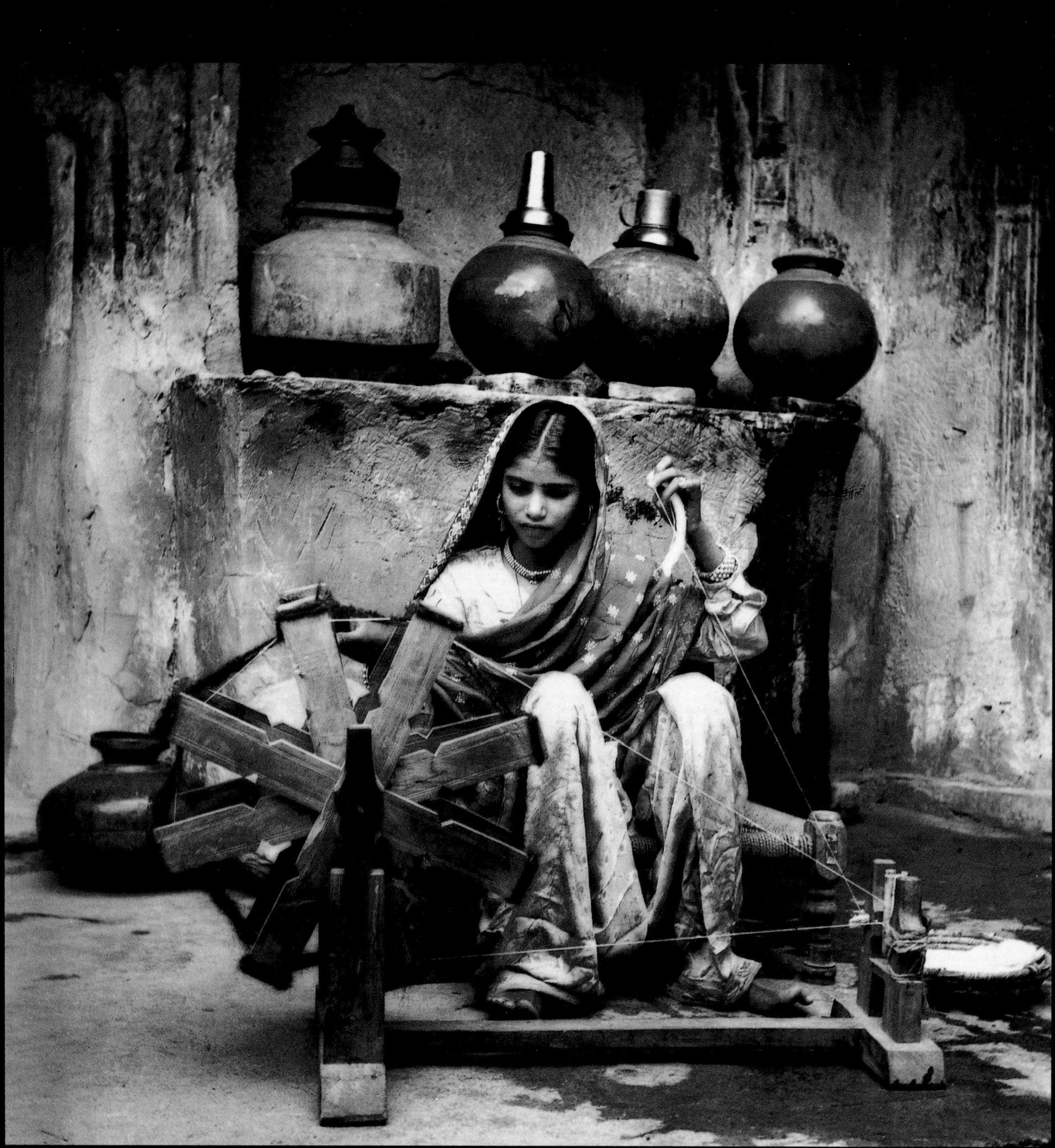

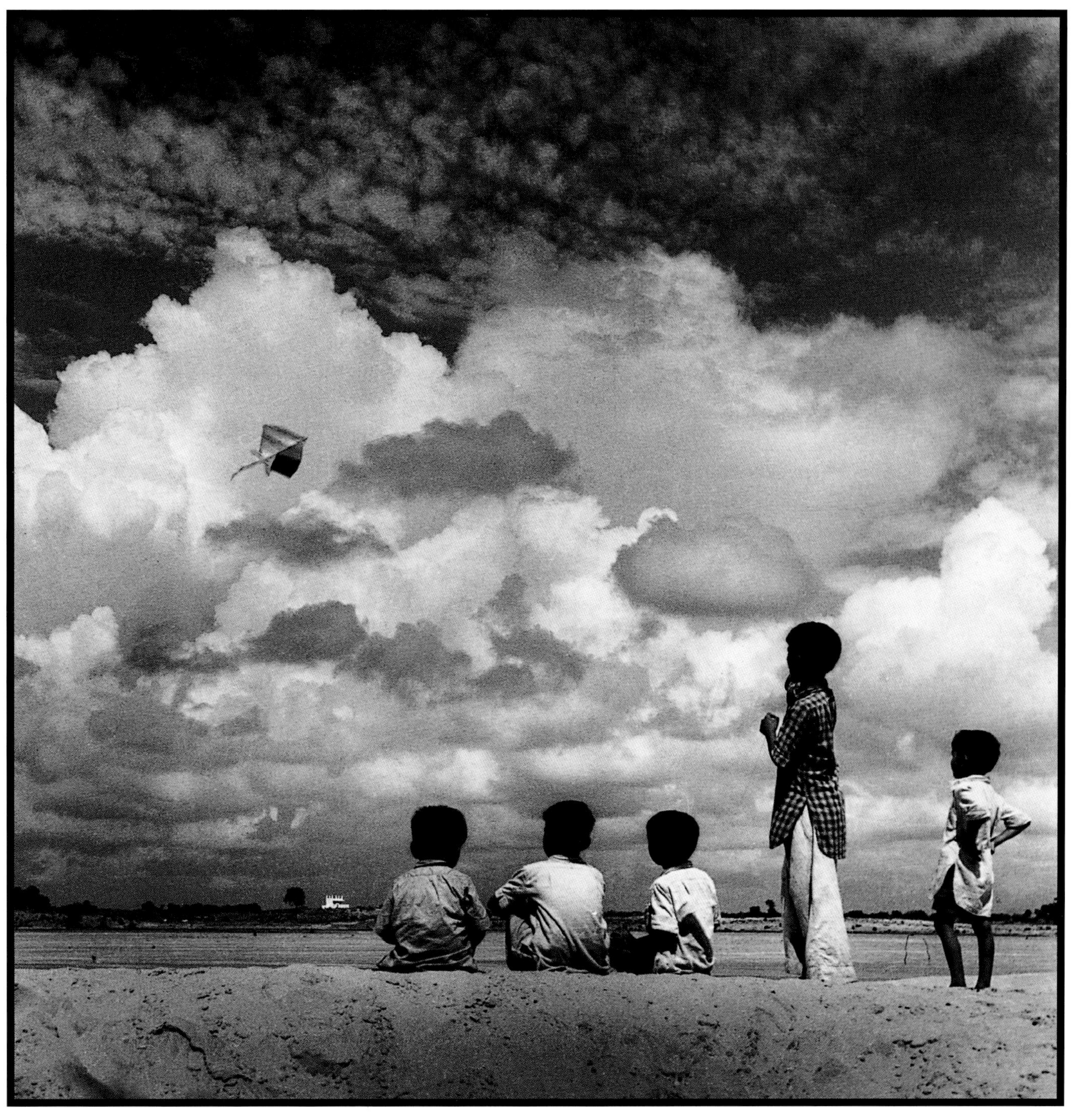

Kite-flying, Rajasthan

Left: 'Work is Worship', Rajasthan

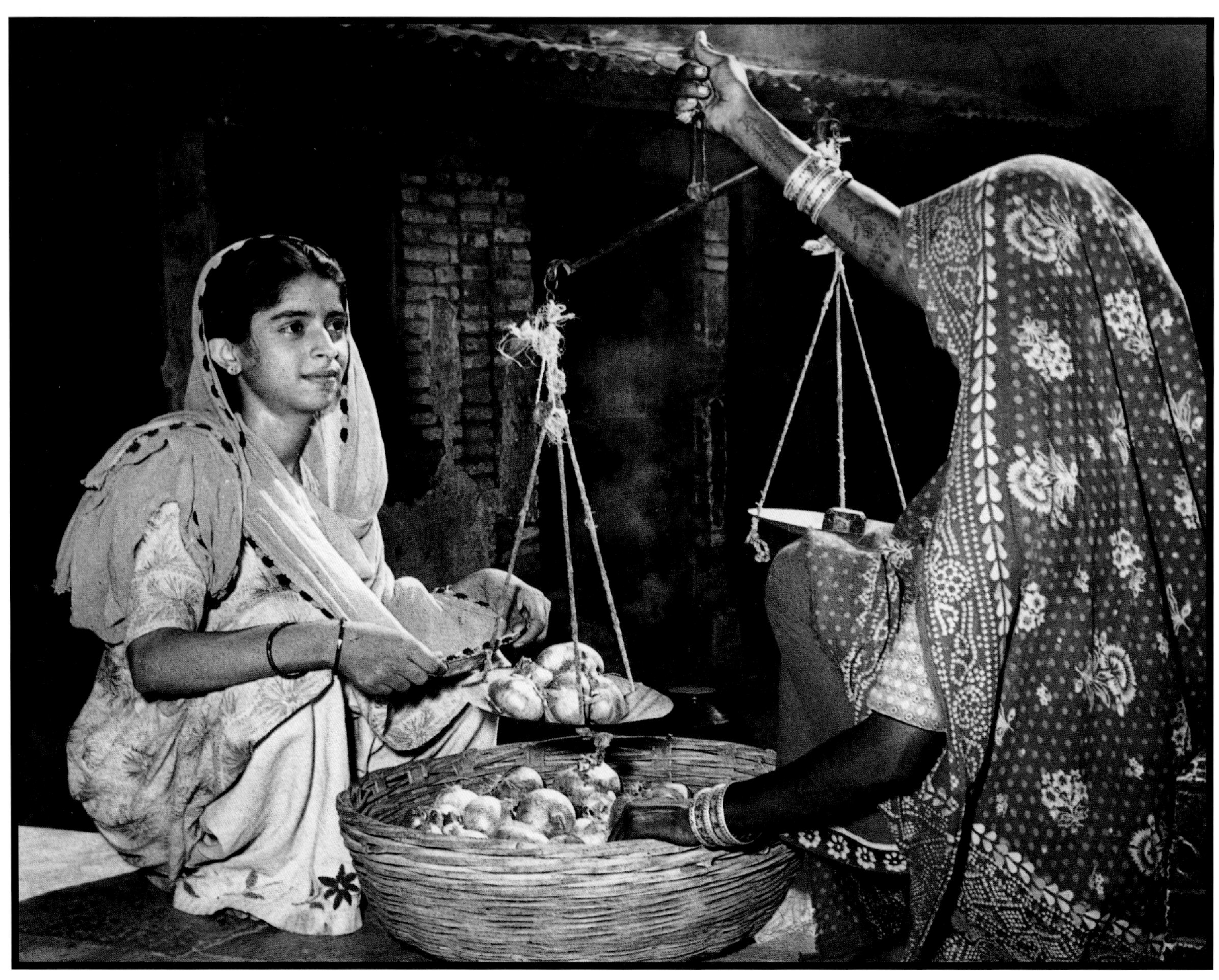

Vegetable vendor, Palanpur

Right: Prayer time, Palanpur

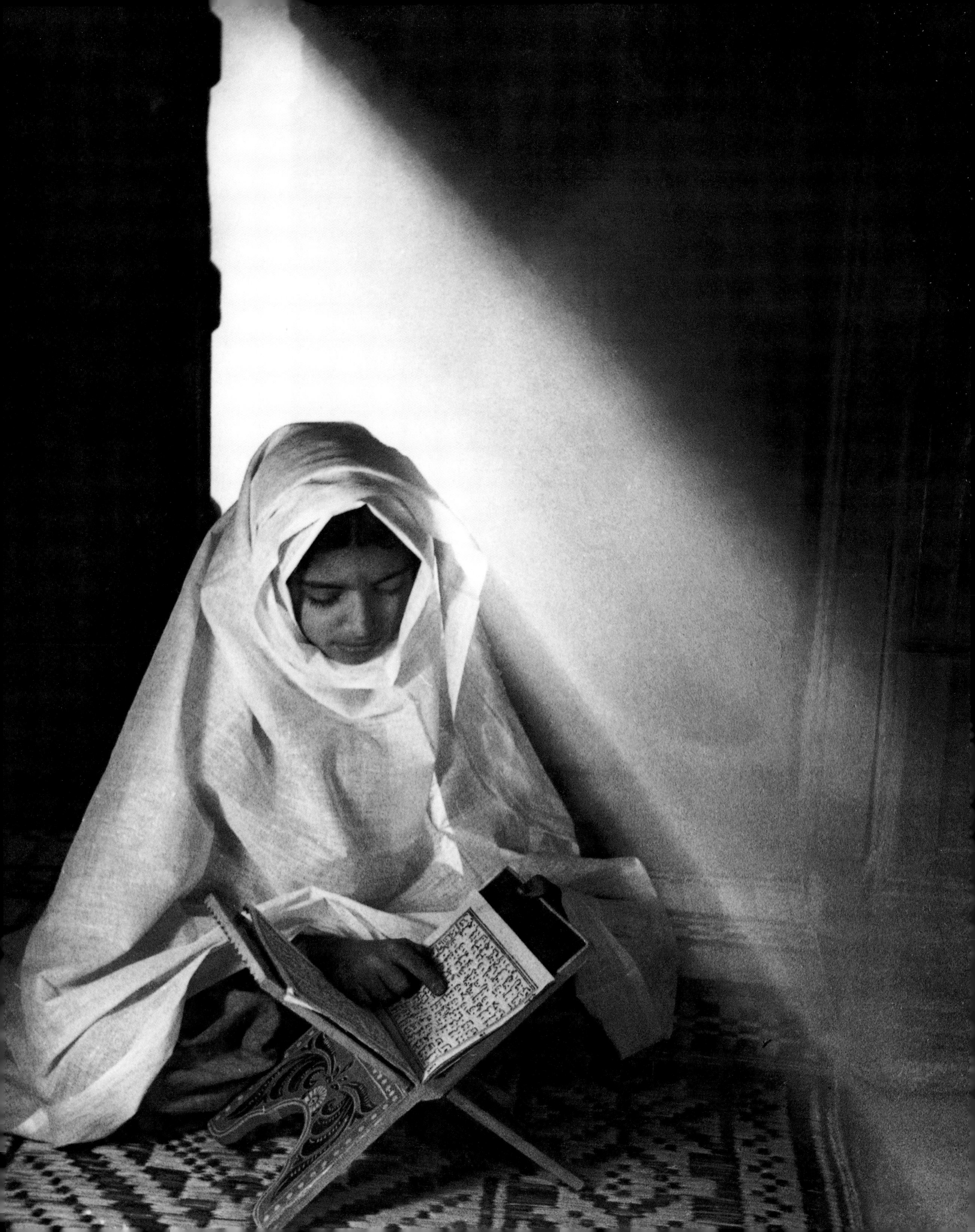

The camel transships people across desolate deserts, but
Mr. A L Syed carried the camel to great heights with his camera.
The camel captivated him right from his first exhibition picture
Traveller of the East. This photograph series depicting different
moods of the desert has become famous under the title Singing
Sands, which is poetry on celluloid.

Though he carved out his position among the 10 best
photographers of the world, his modesty made him a legend in his
own lifetime. In an interview, when asked how he could click with
his trembling hands and produce marvels in spite of Parkinson's
disease, he quoted the poet Simab:

> *Main to kuchh bhi nahi hum, Simab*
> *Bat meri mere sarkar bana dete hain.*
>
> (I am nobody, Simab, but
> My Lord coaxes me to be someone.)

And the demonstration! It was another marvel.

Sanat Shukla
Correspondent, *Times of India*, Palanpur

Right: Desert child, Rajasthan

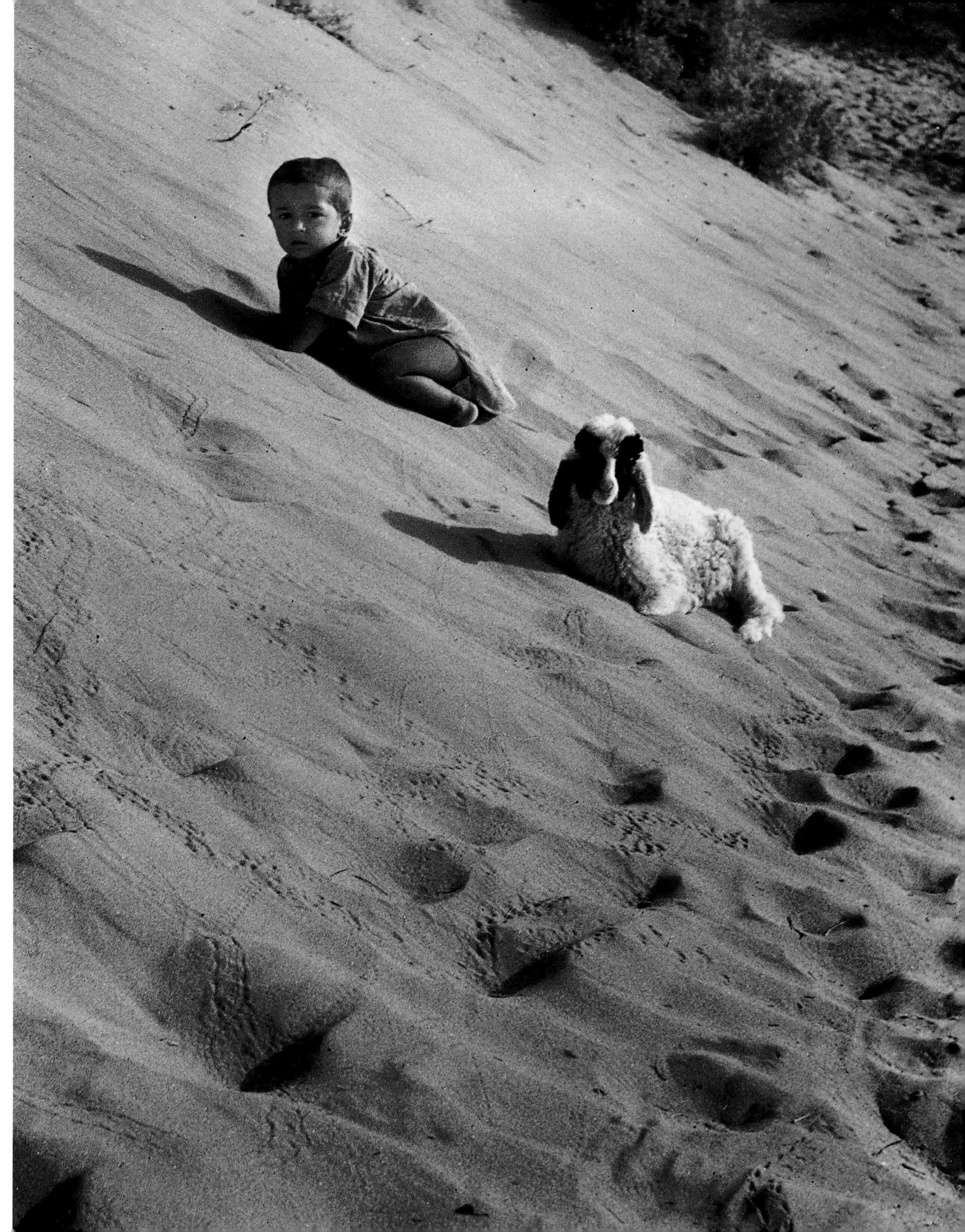

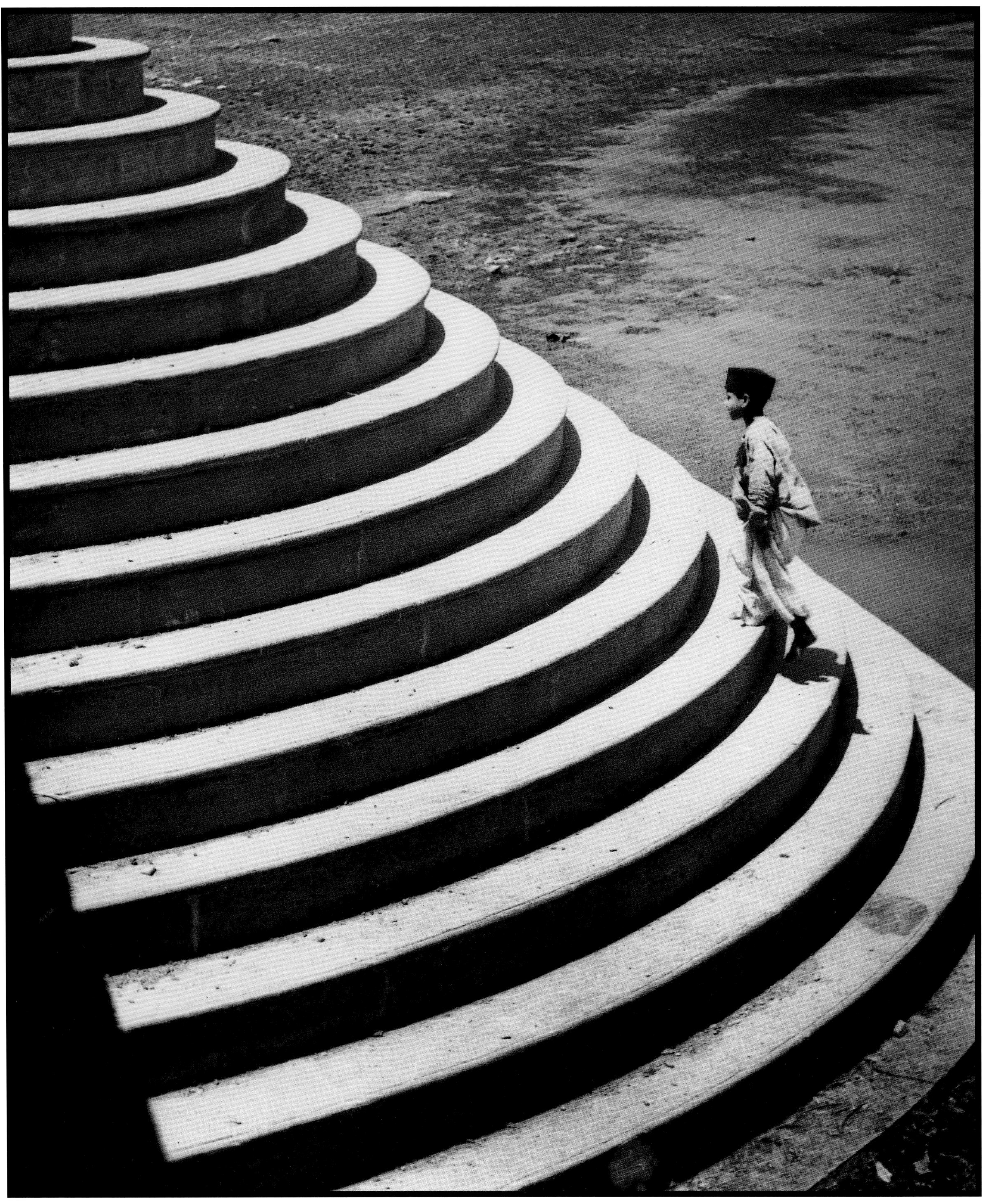

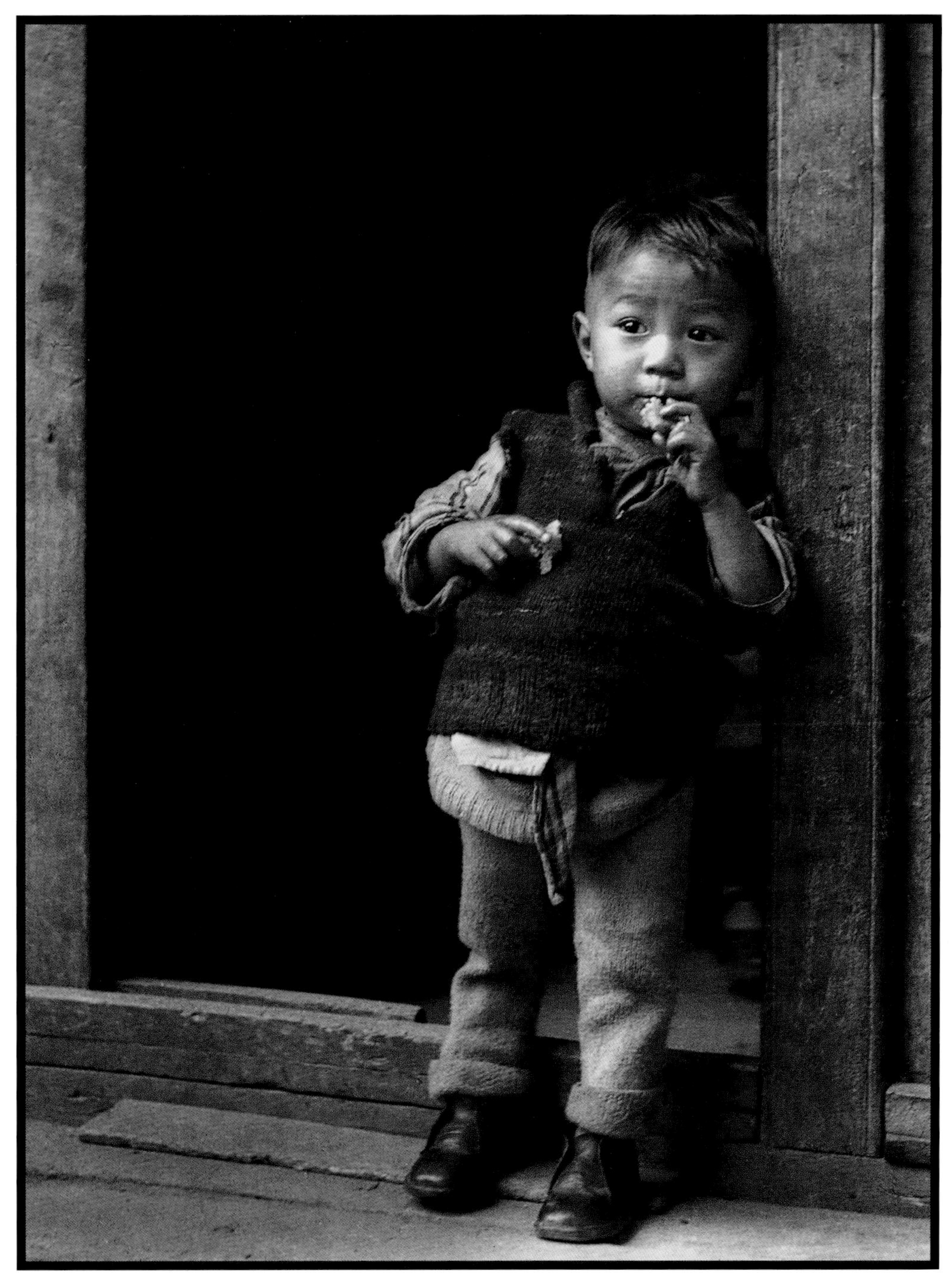

Nepali boy, Darjeeling

Left: Steps and steps, Udaipur

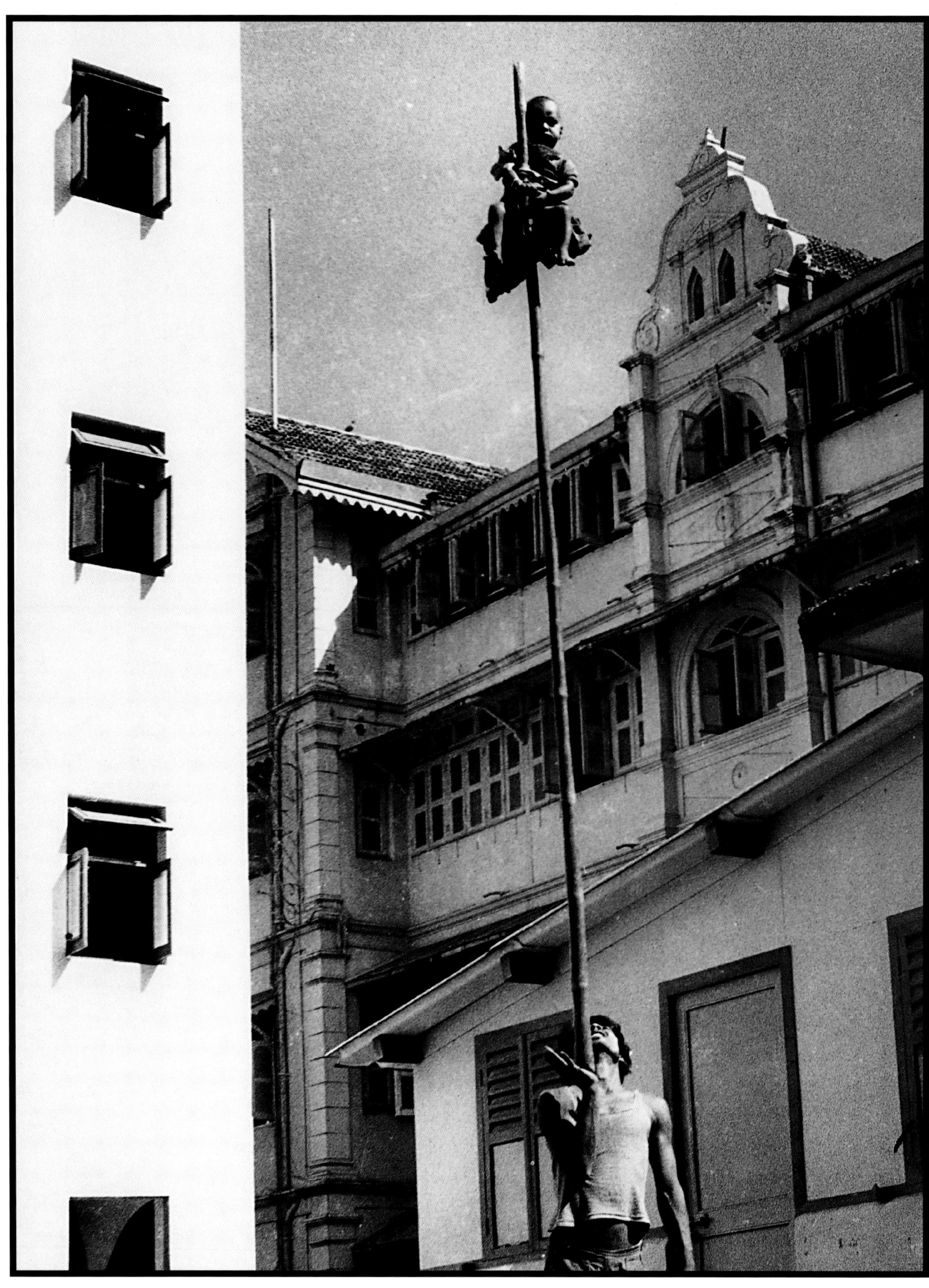

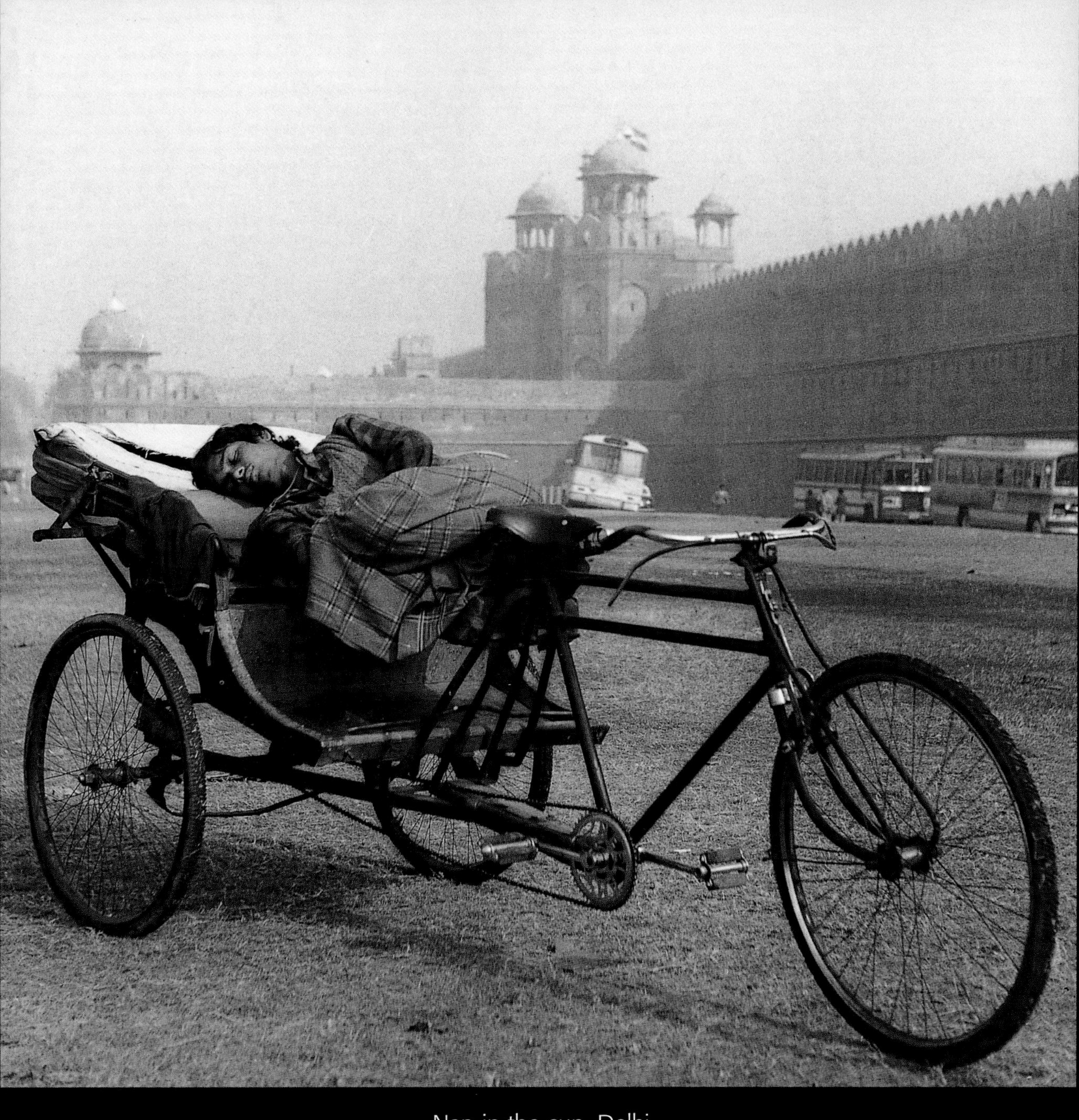

Nap in the sun, Delhi

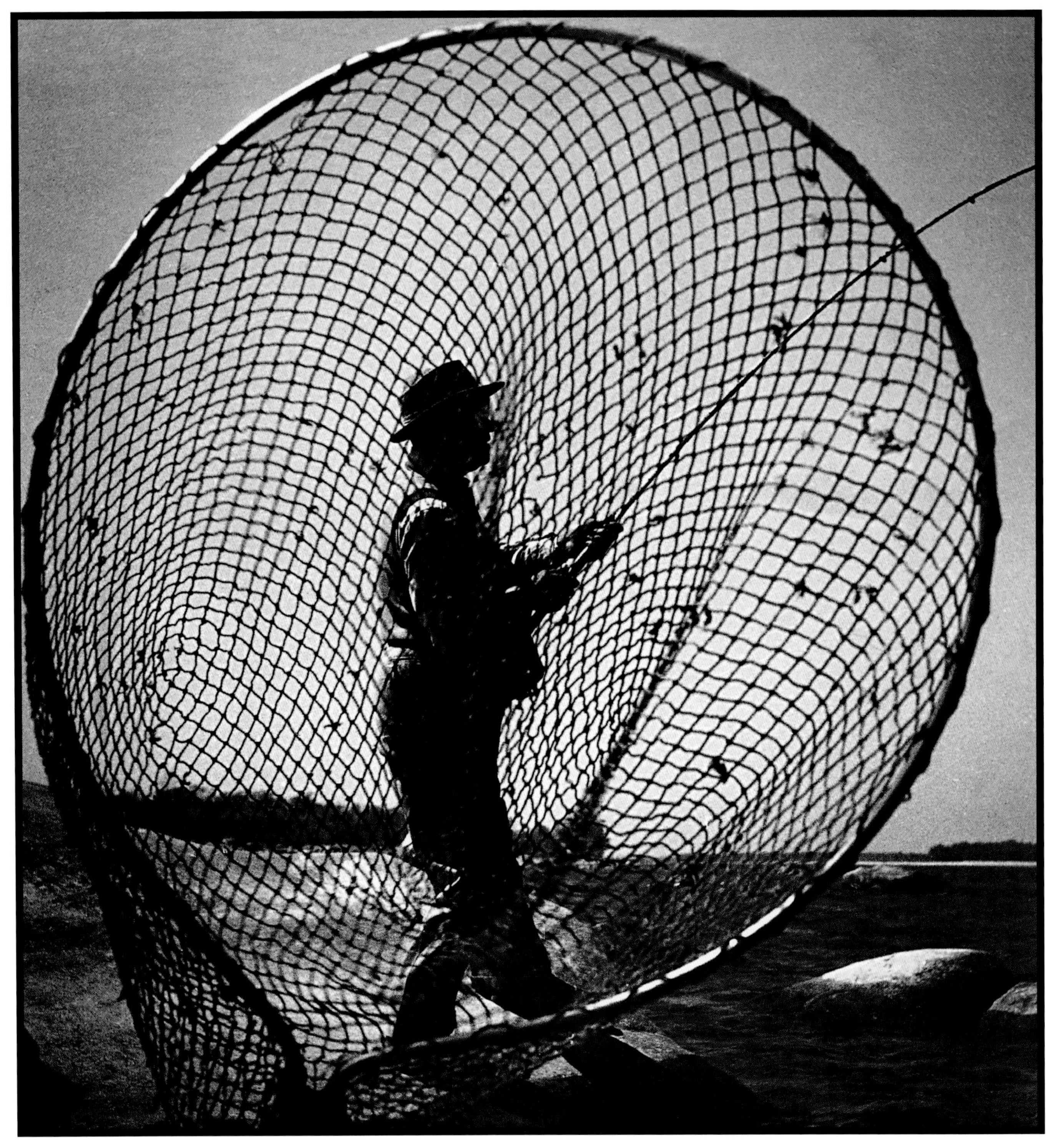

The angler, Bhopal

Right: In the Garden of Fountains, Udaipur

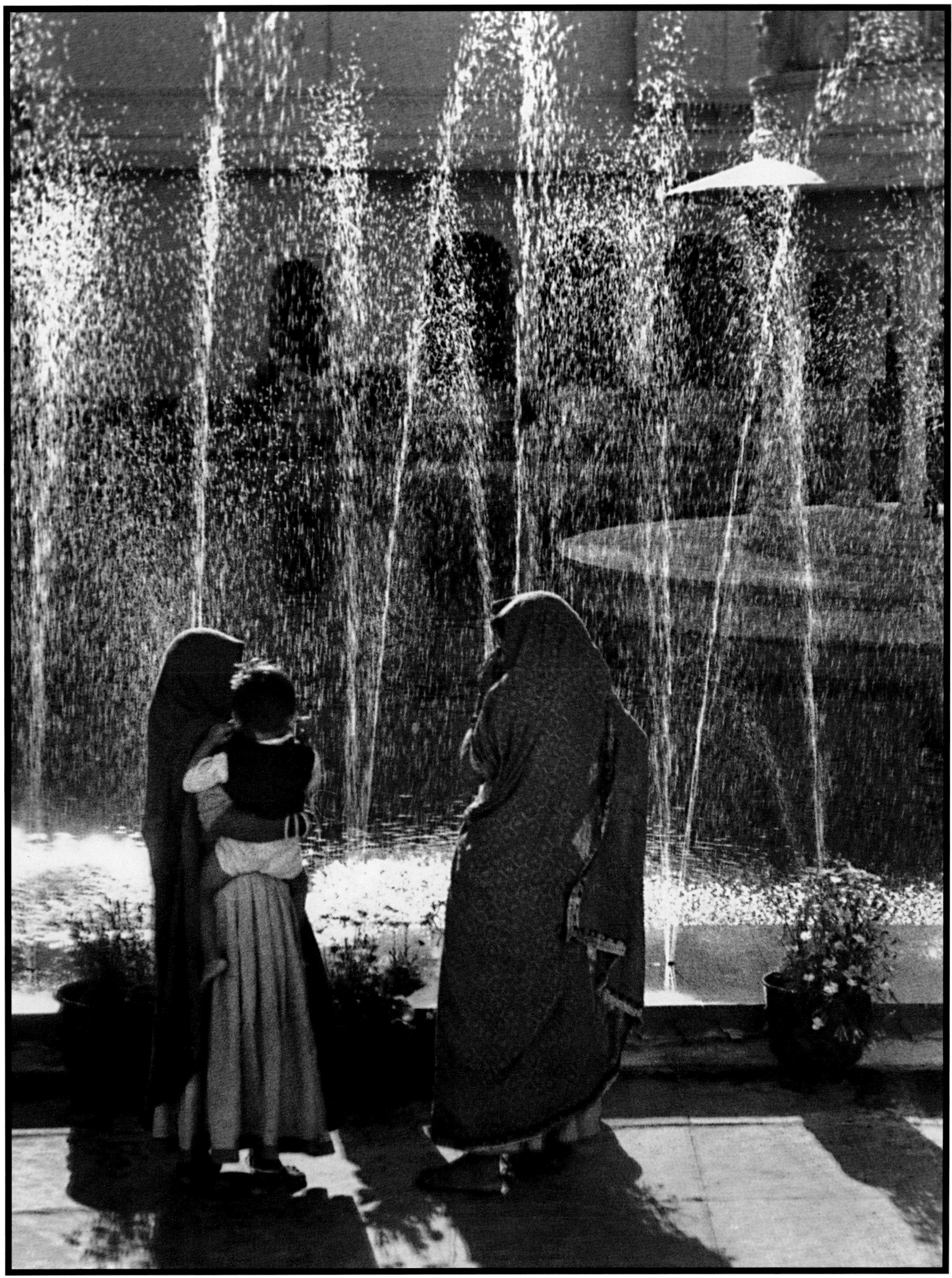

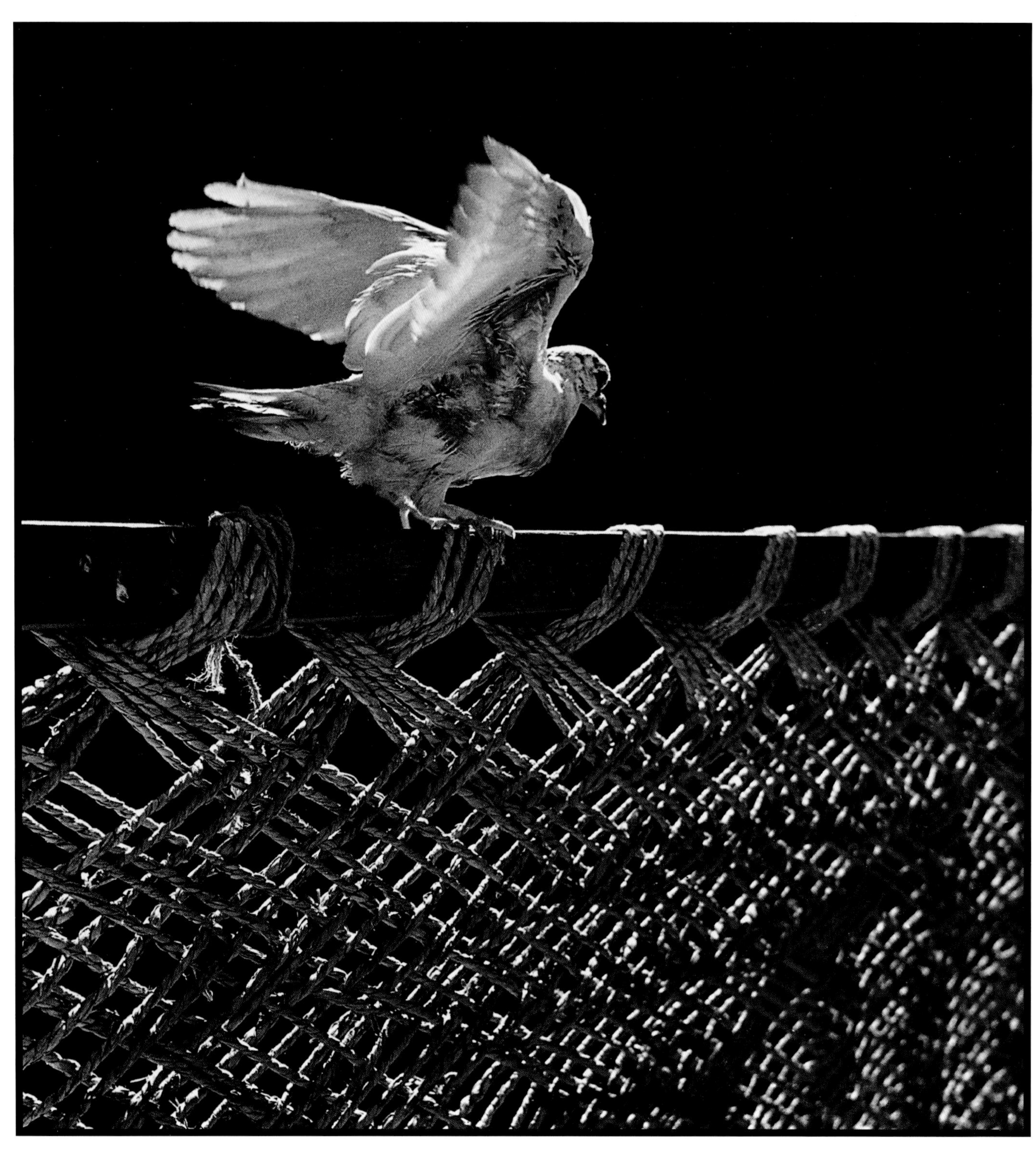

Before they catch me, Palanpur

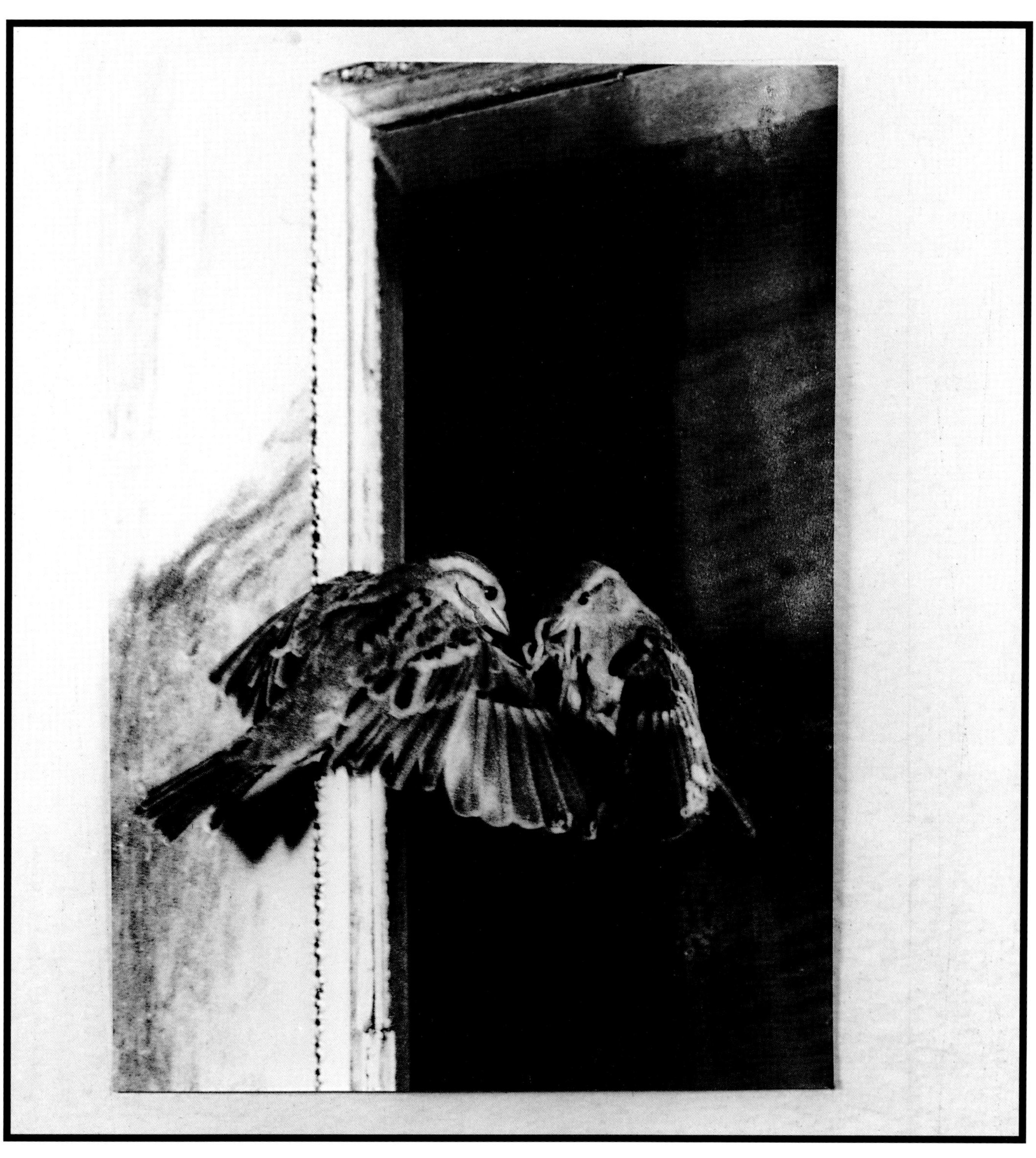

Envious, Palanpur

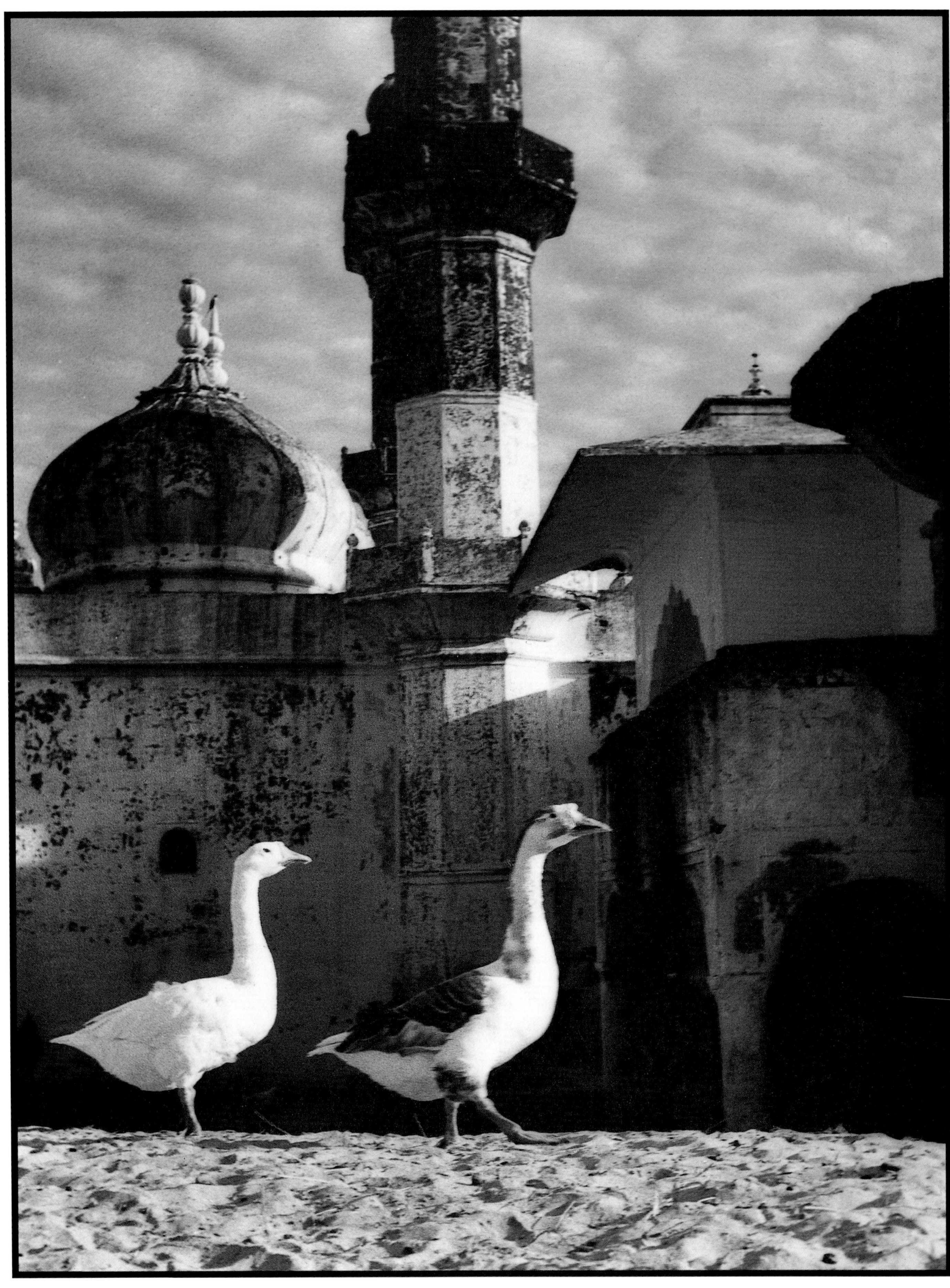

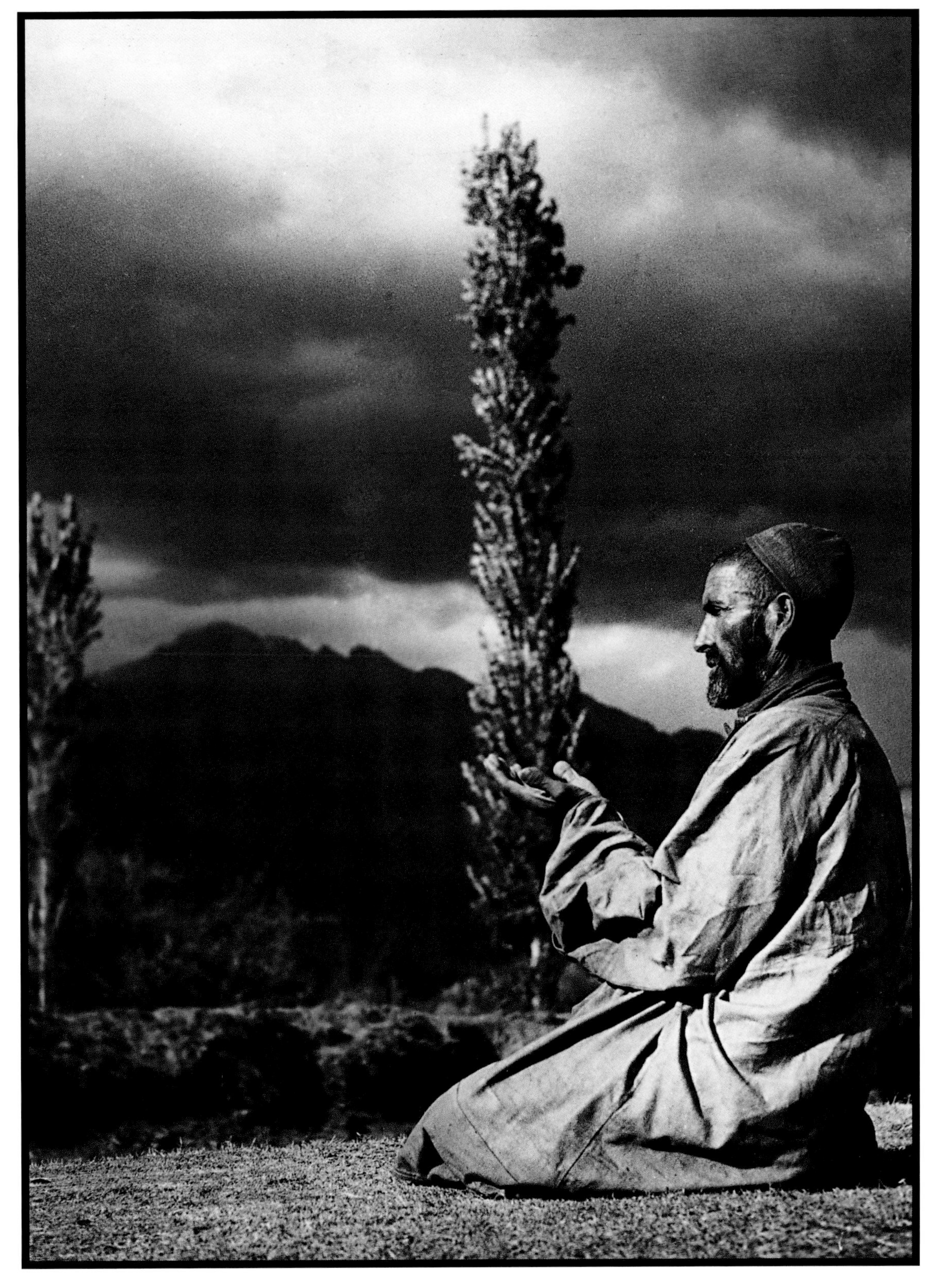

Evening prayer, Kashmir

Left: Let us go now, Hasteela, Rajasthan

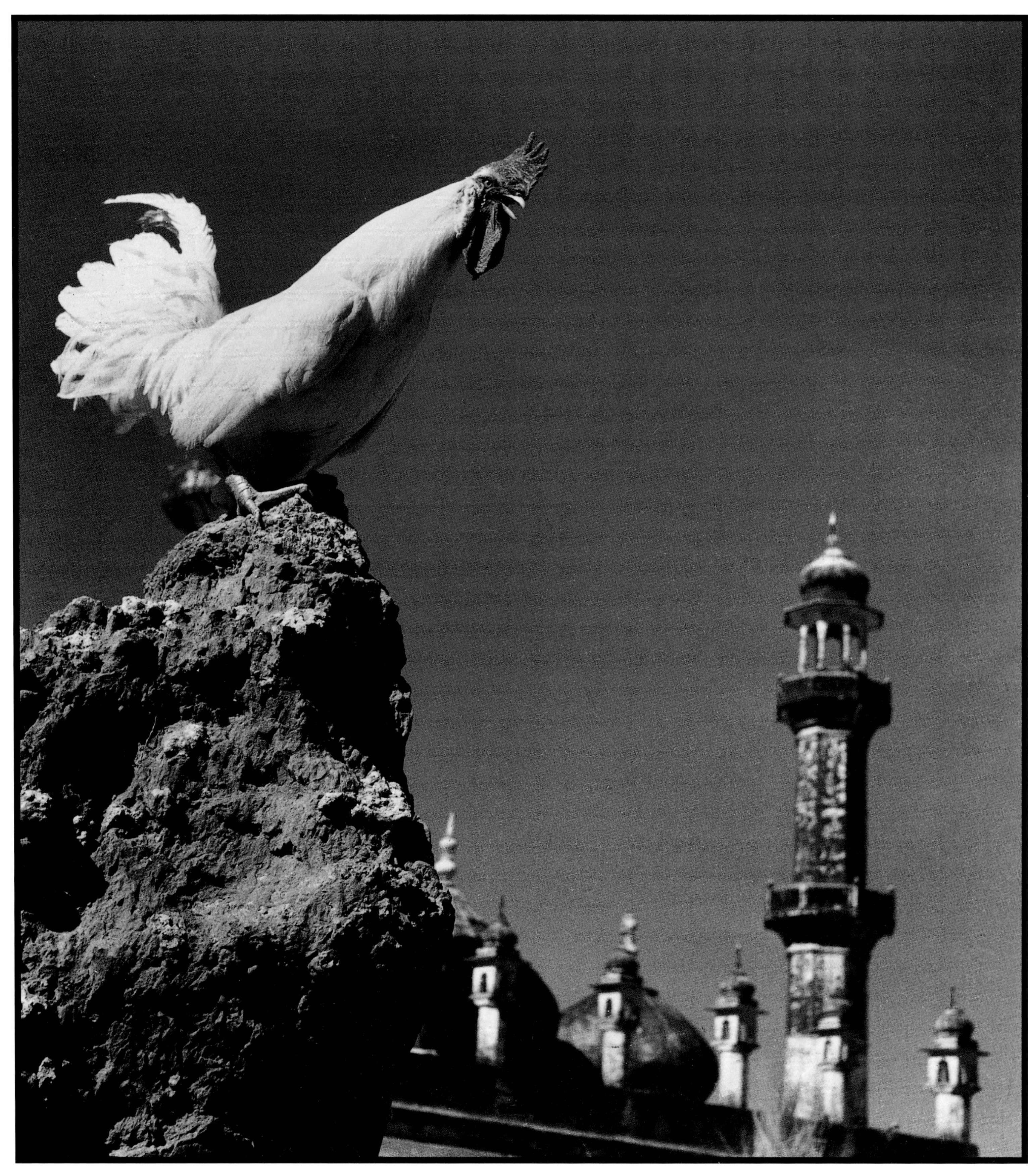

Morning prayer, Hasteela, Rajasthan

Right: The Rajput of Dungarpur

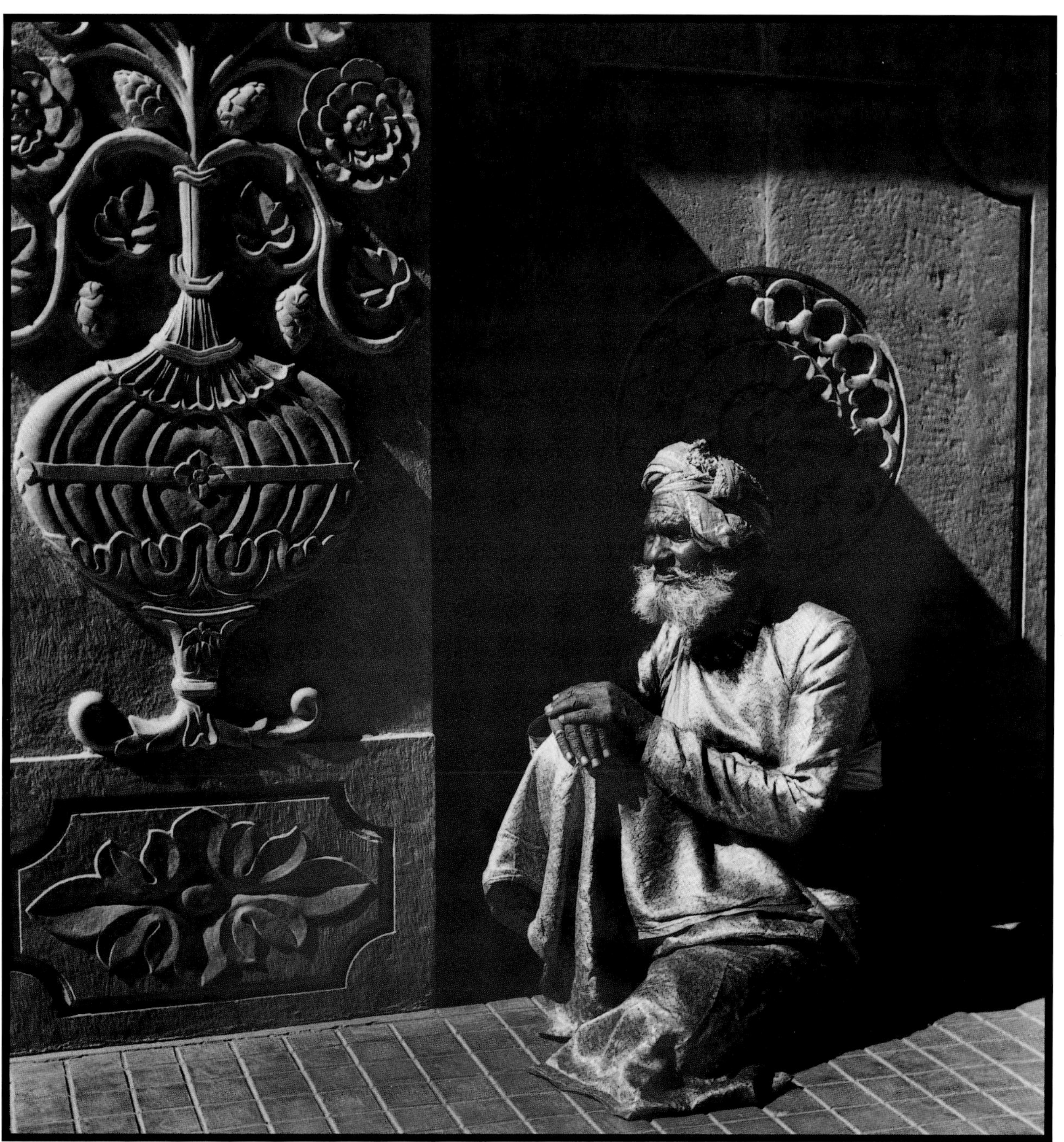

I knew A L Syed from the early days of my life. He visited Dungarpur on all the important occasions in my family between 1940 and 1955. My revered father the late Maharawal Laxman Singhji sahib and other relatives considered him almost as a member of the family. For me his memory will remain everlasting.

H H Maharawal Mahipal Singh of Dungarpur

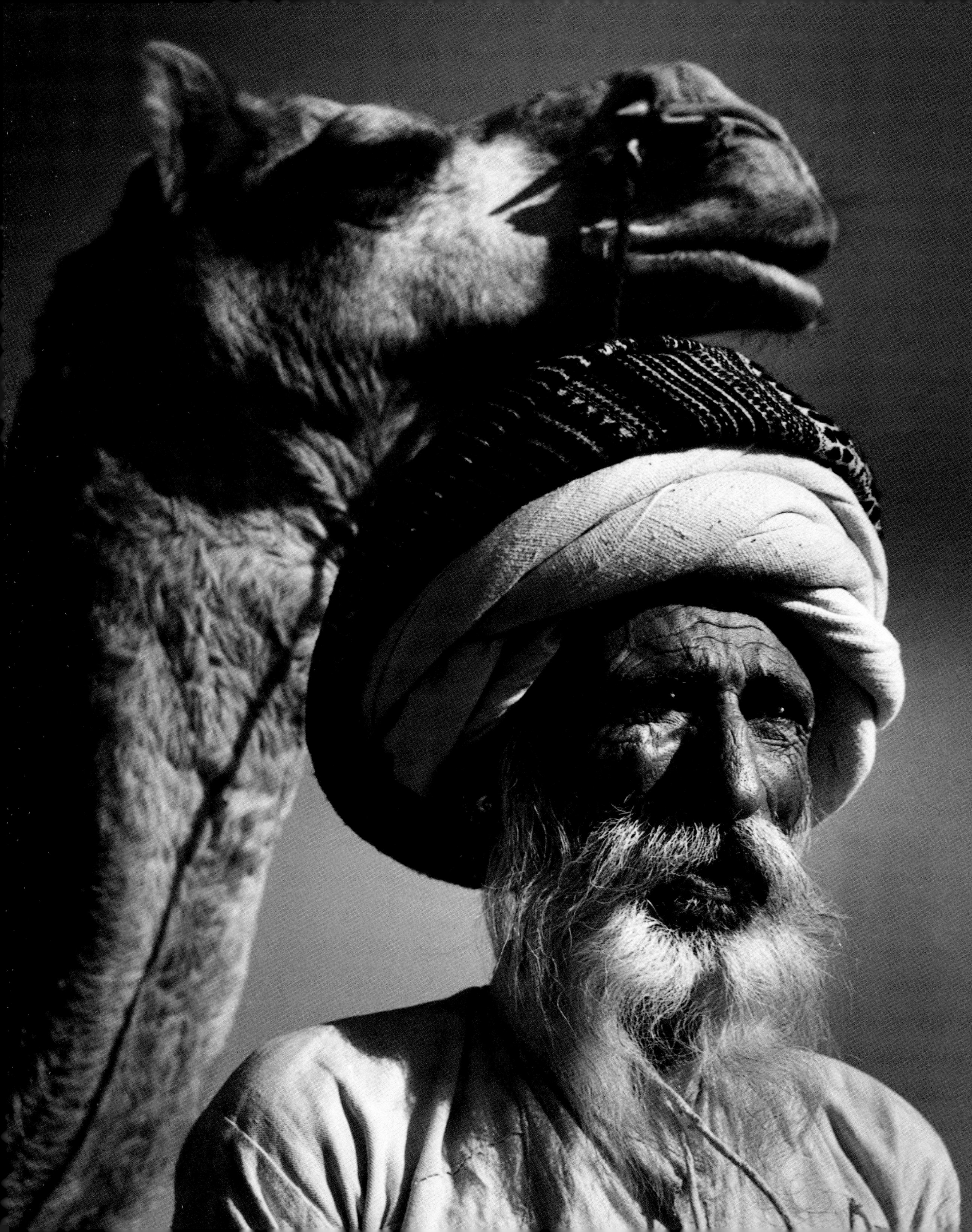

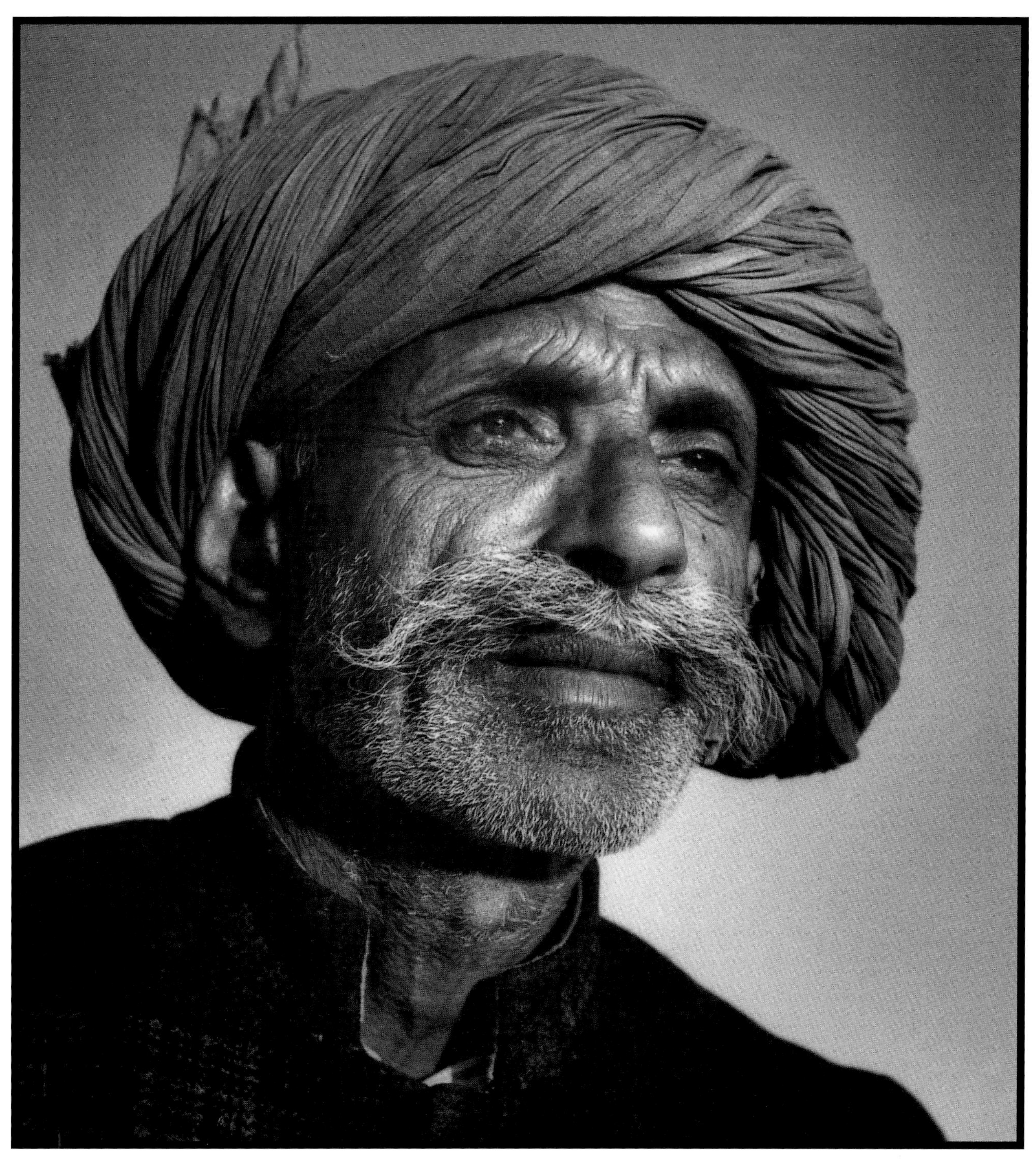

Sarpanch, village leader, Gujarat

Left: Behold the desert

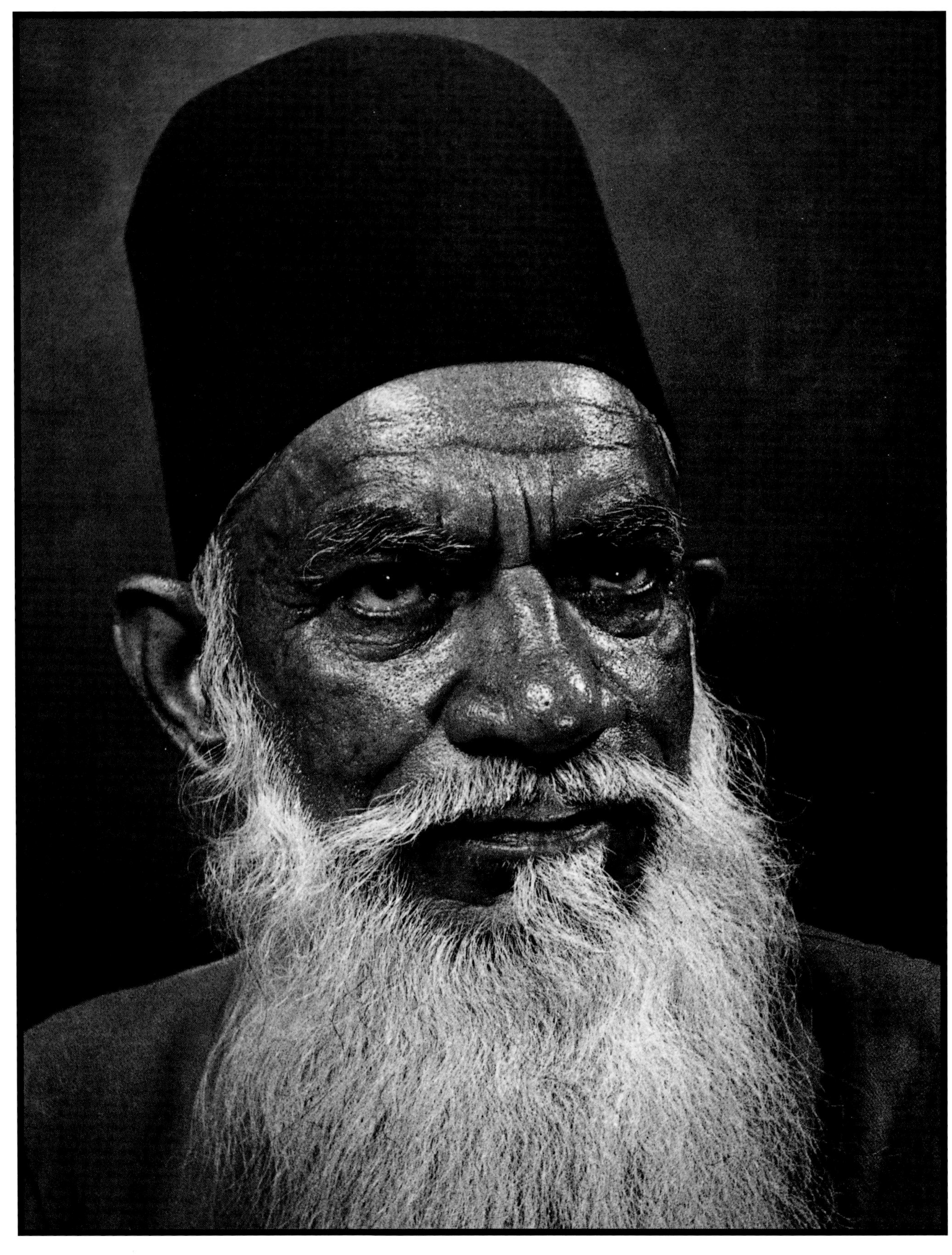

The far-away look

Right: Poojari, priest

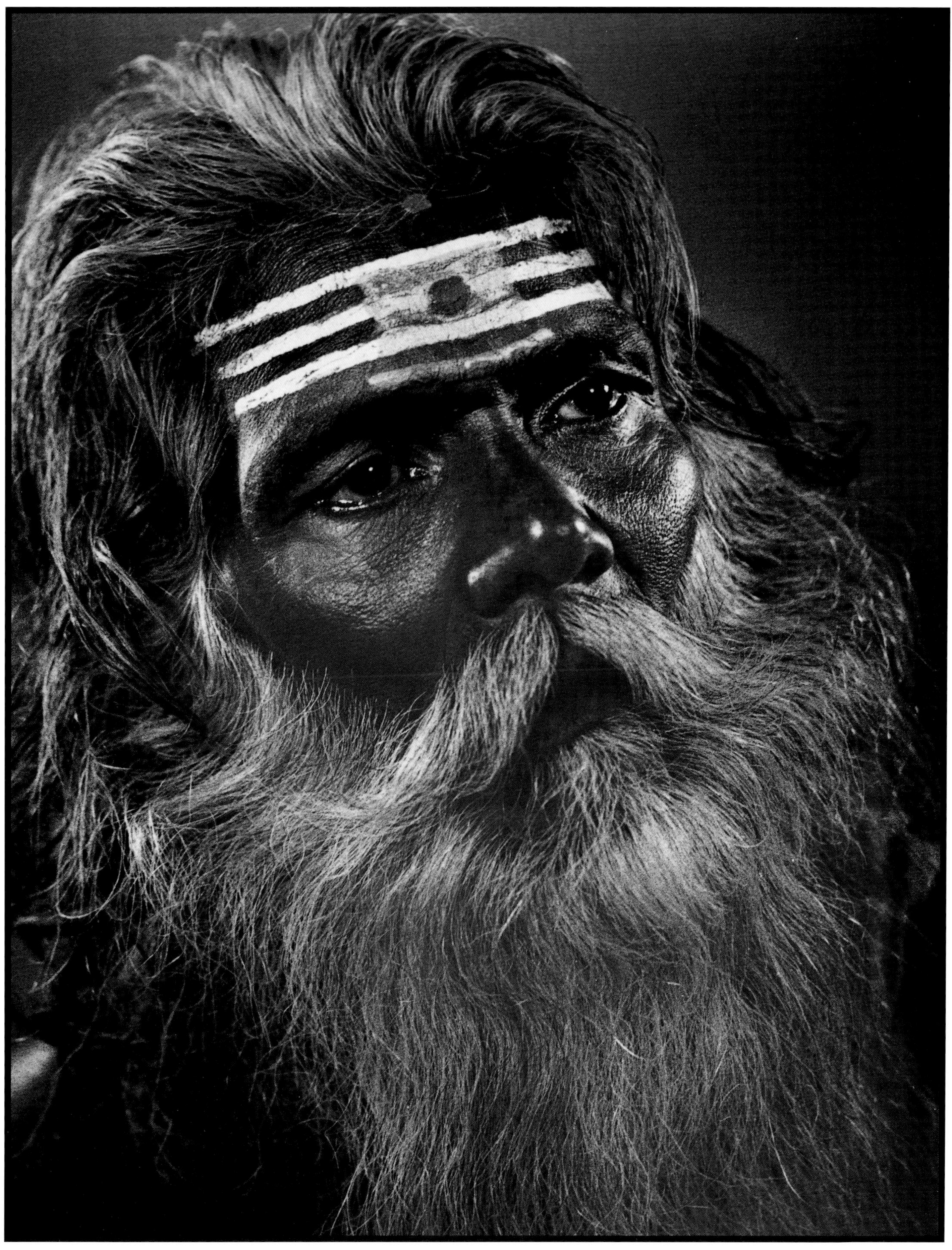

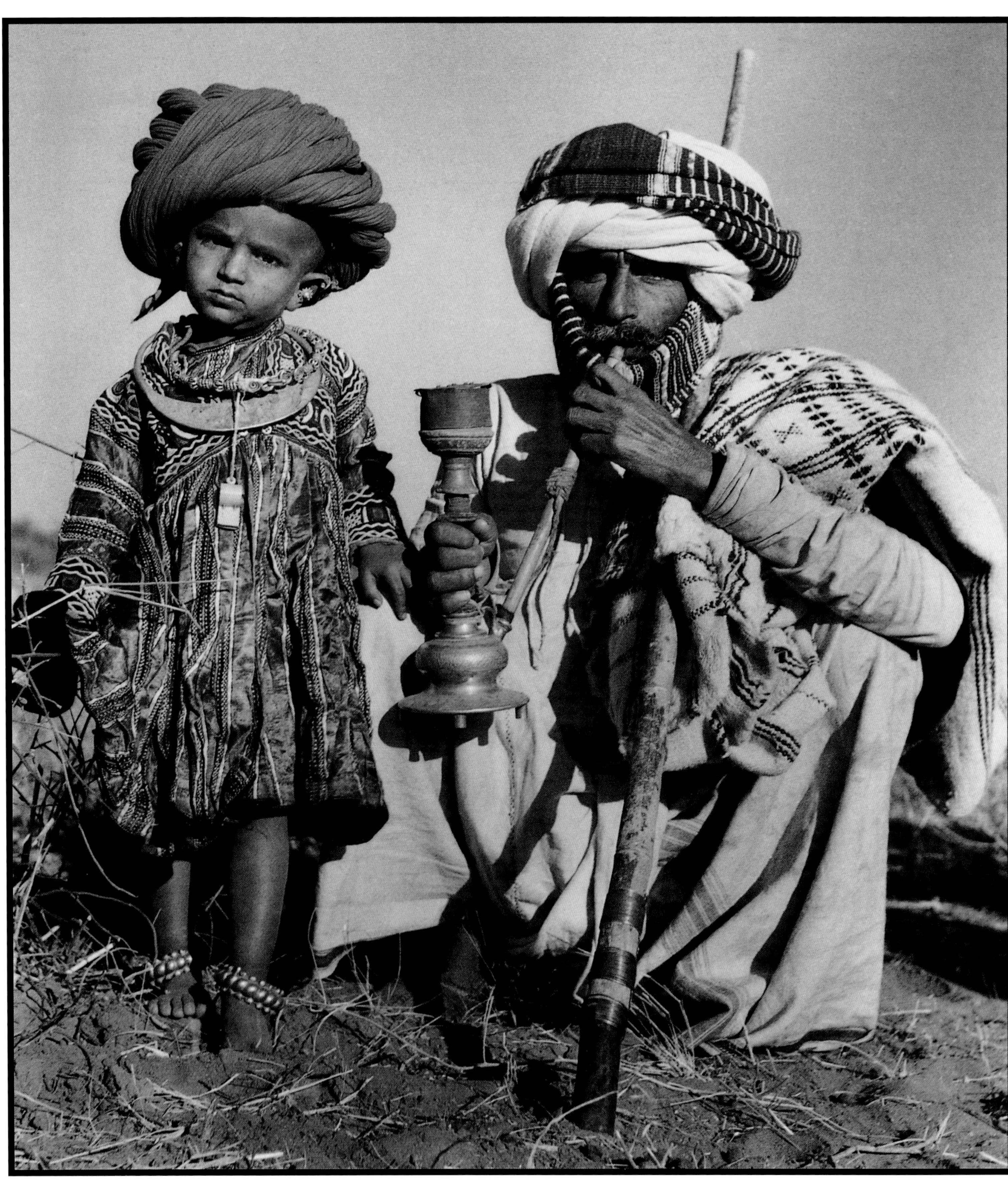

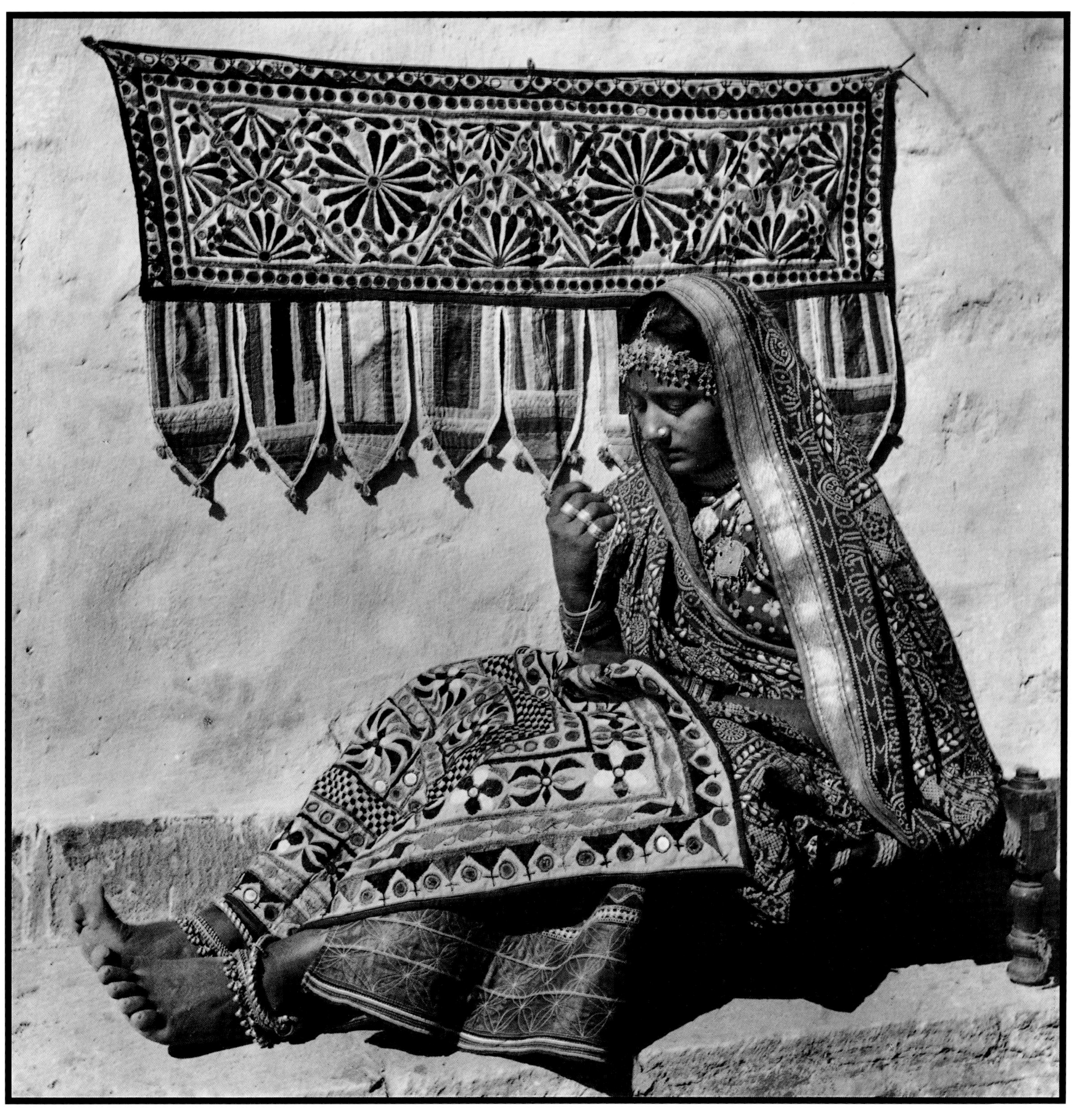

Artisan of Kachchh, Gujarat

Left: Kachchhi father and son, Kachchh

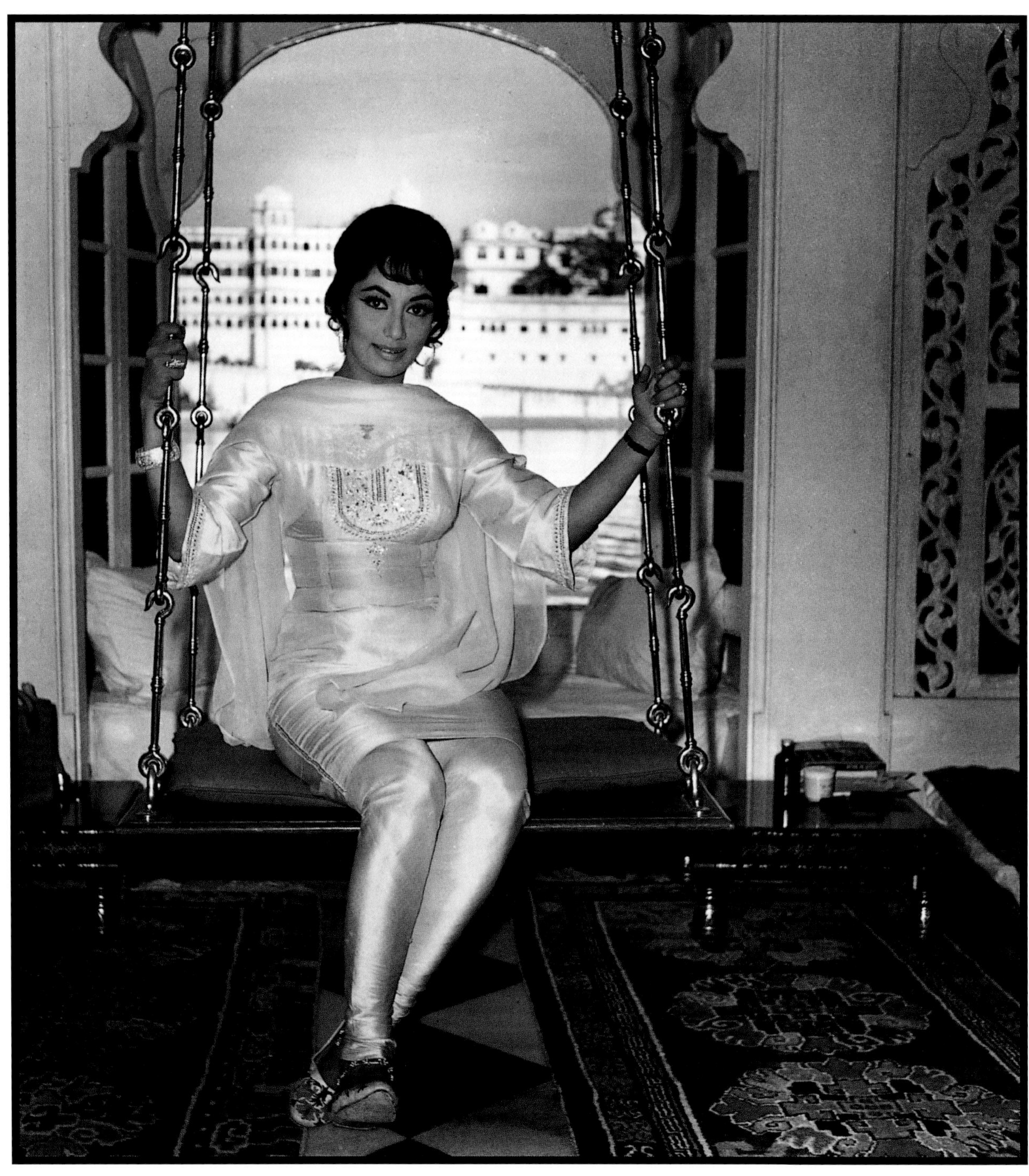

Sadhana, film actress, Lake Palace, Udaipur

Right: Saira Banu, film actress

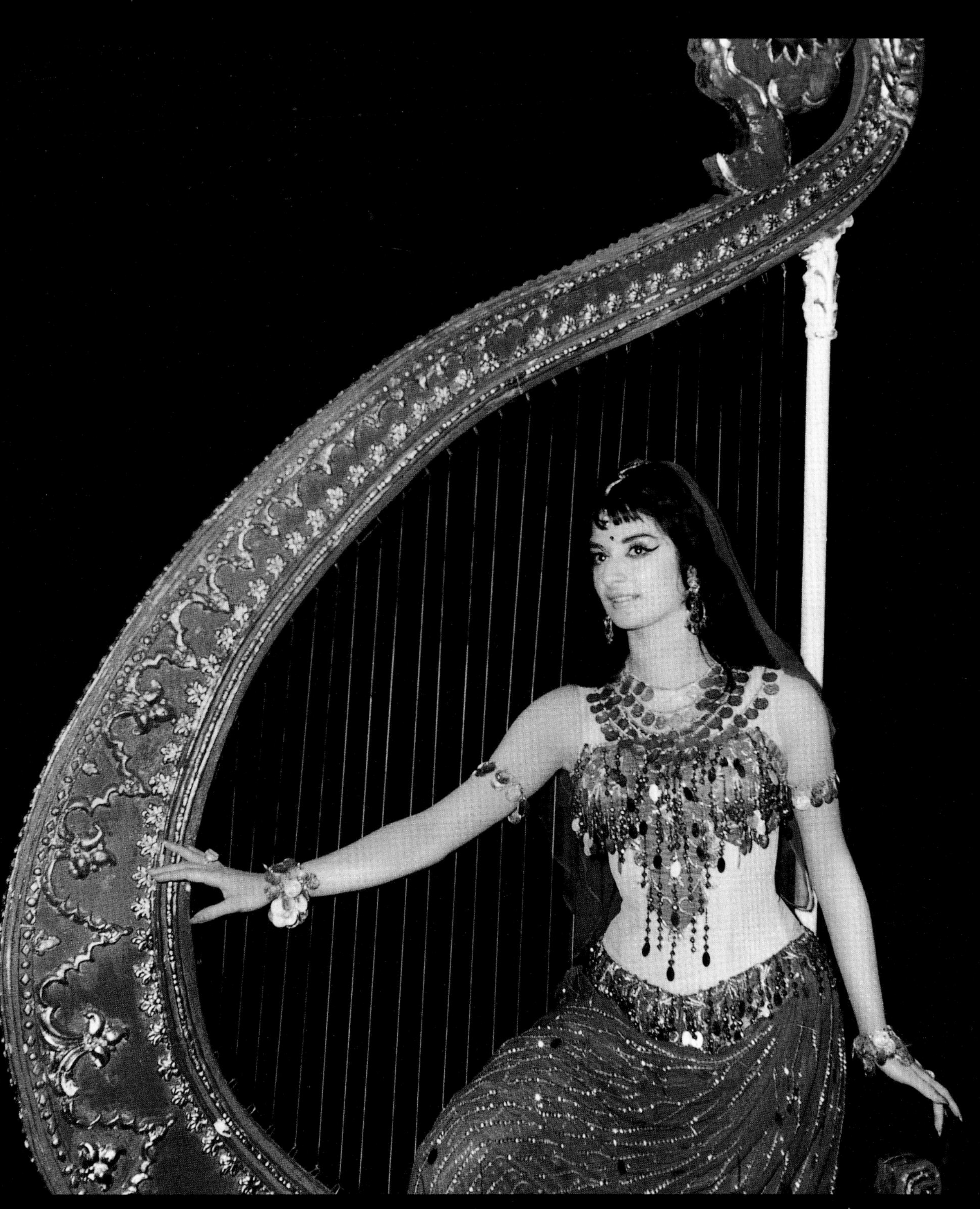

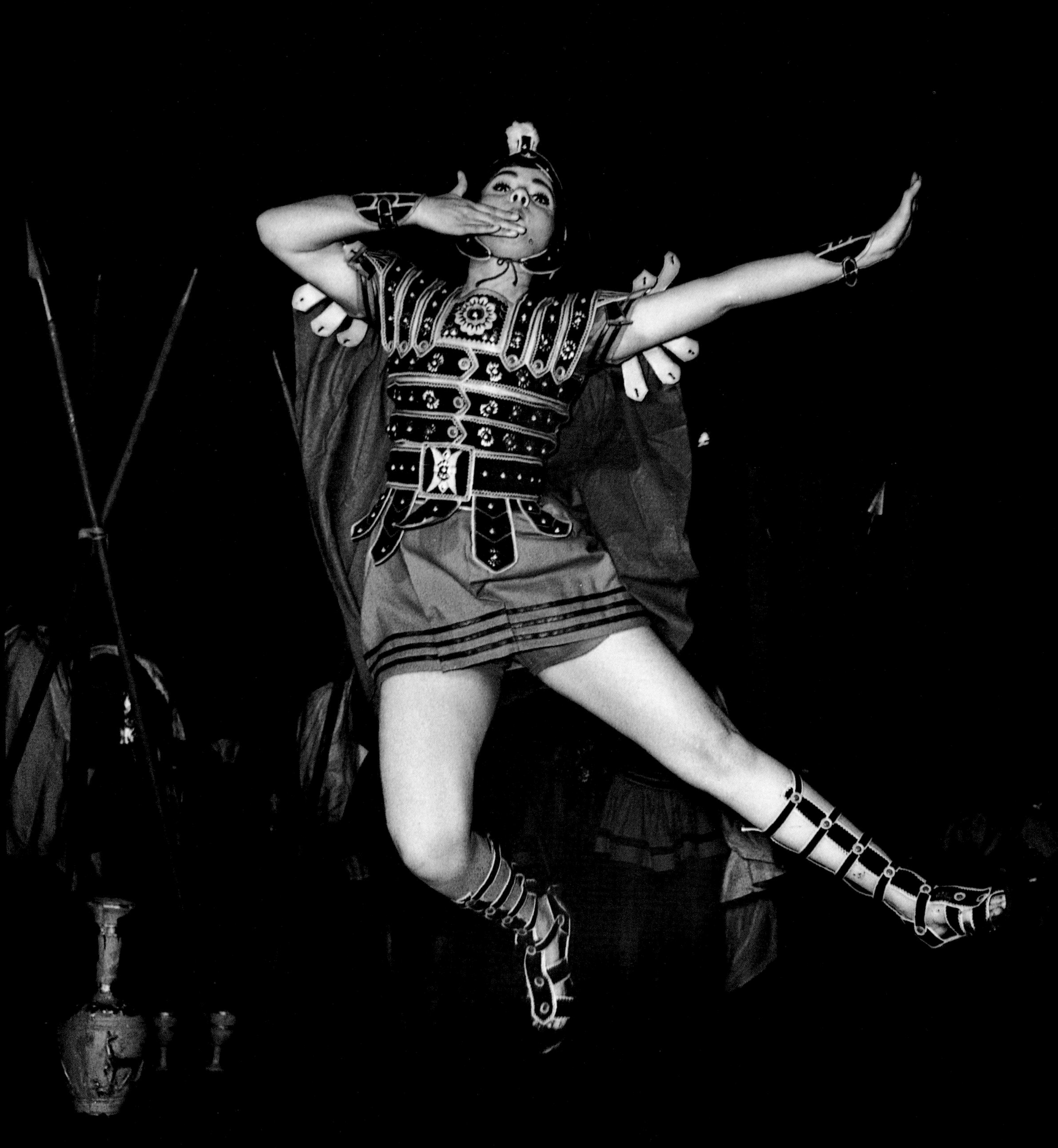

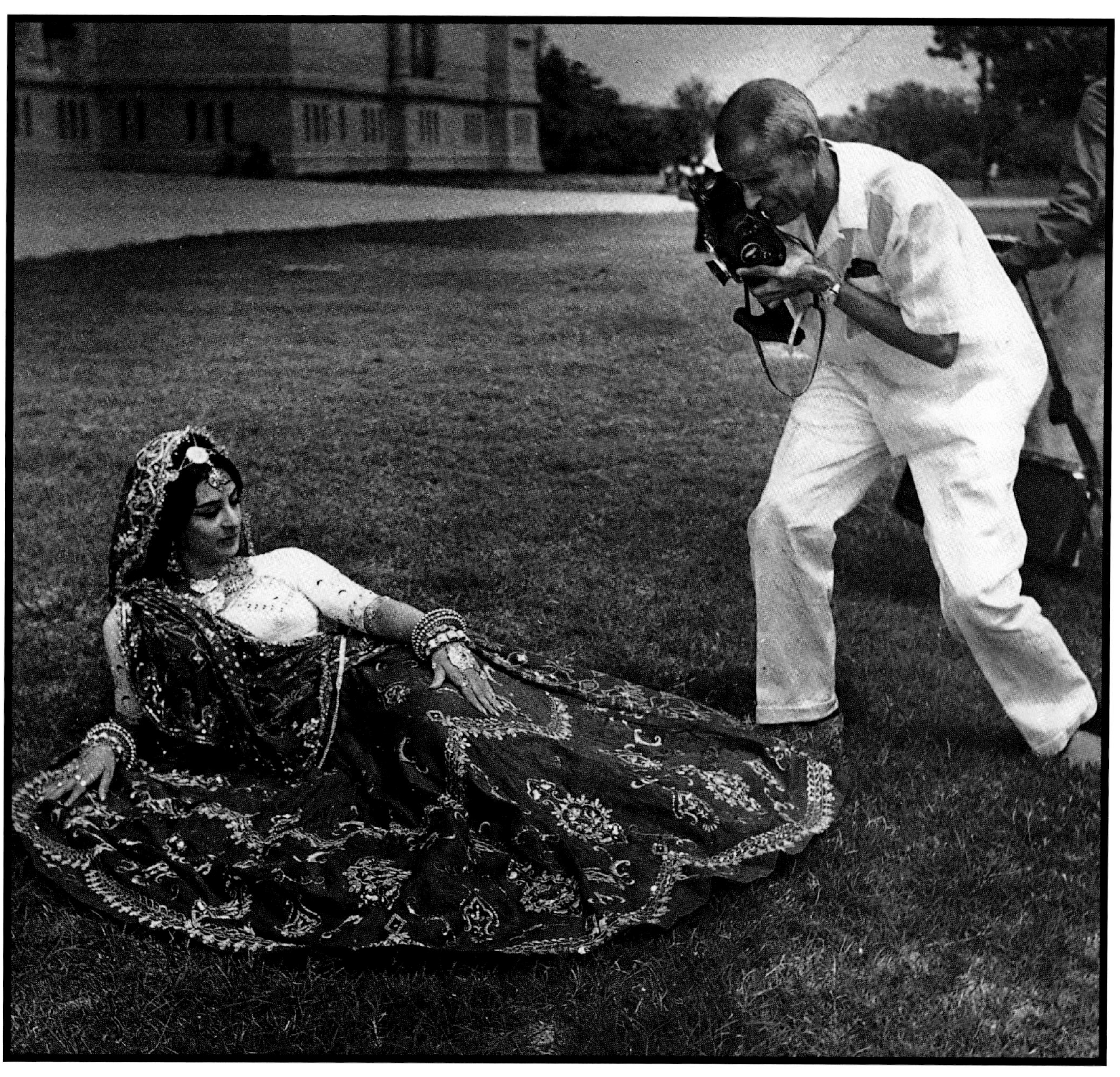

Saira Banu and A L Syed, Umaid Bhavan, Jodhpur

Left: Mumtaz, film actress

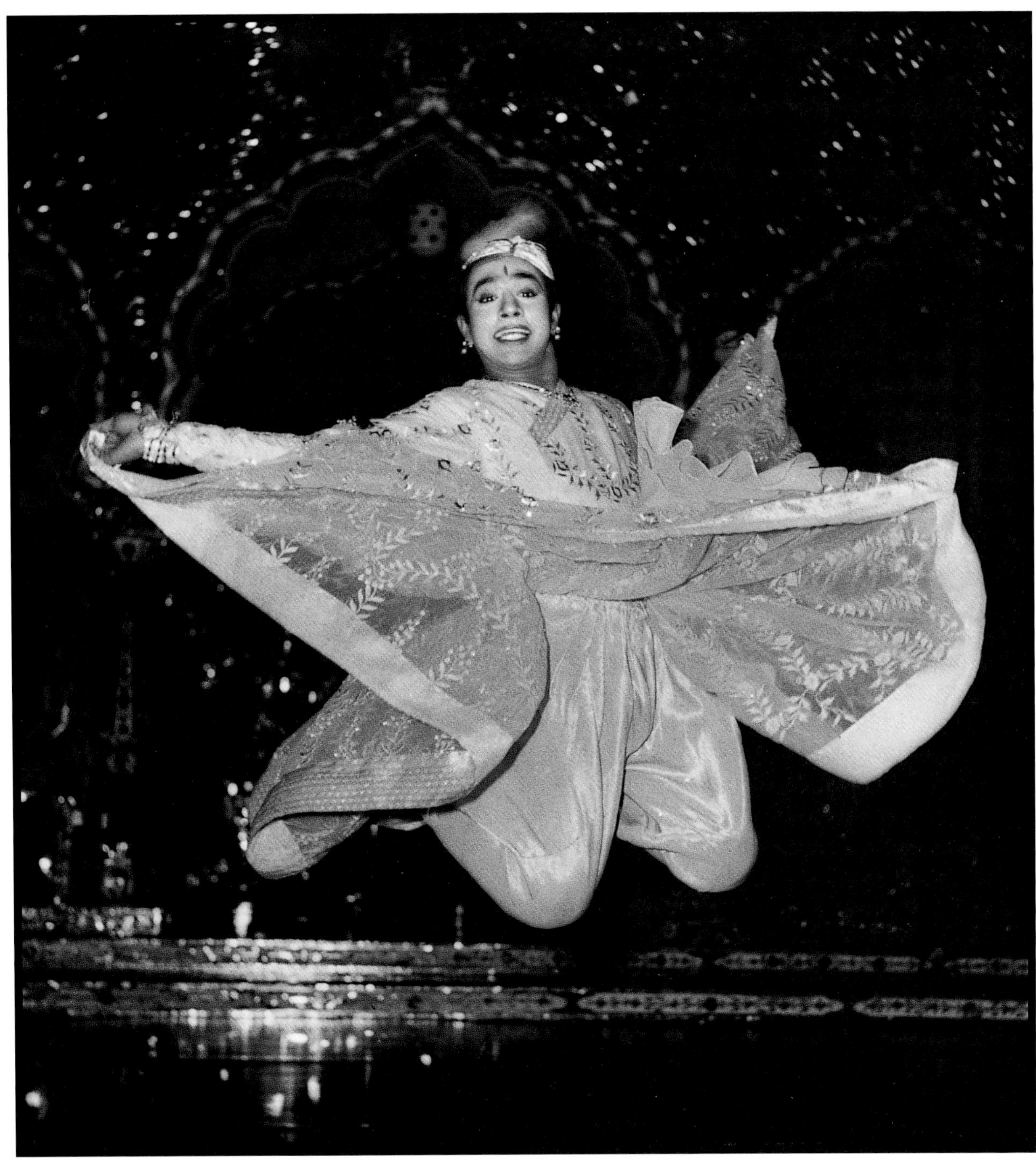

Gopi Krishna, dancer

Right: Sunil Dutt, film actor

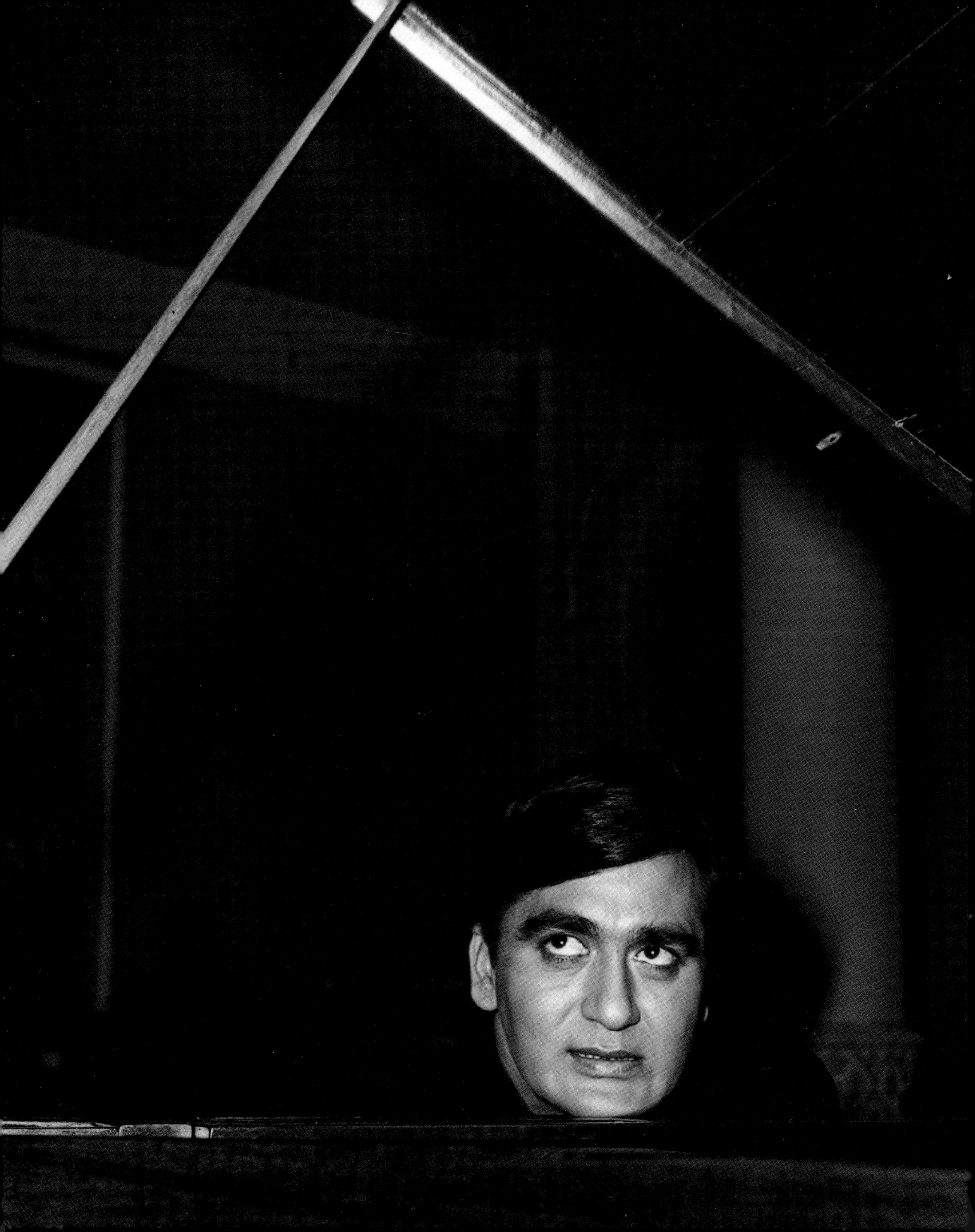

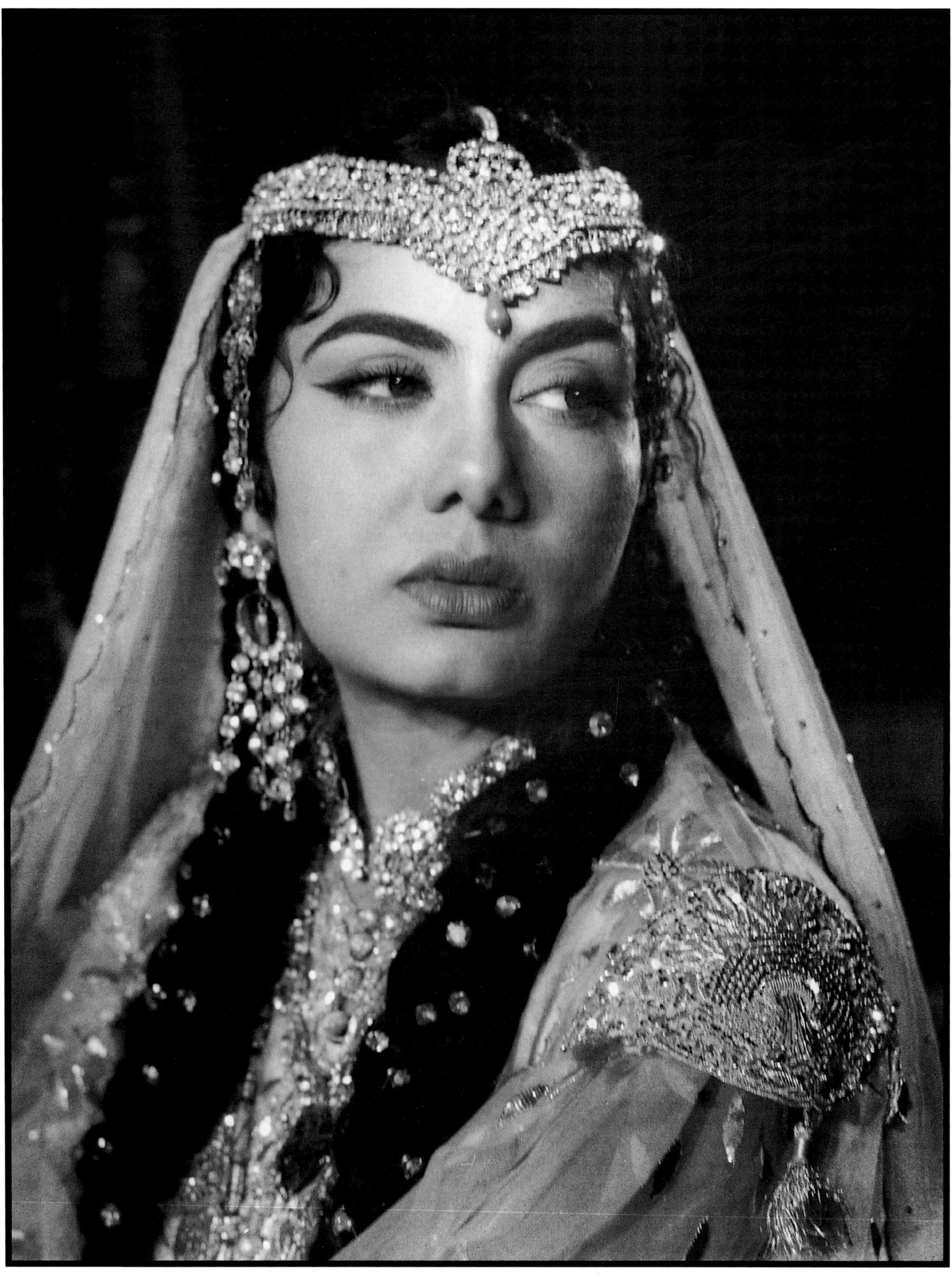

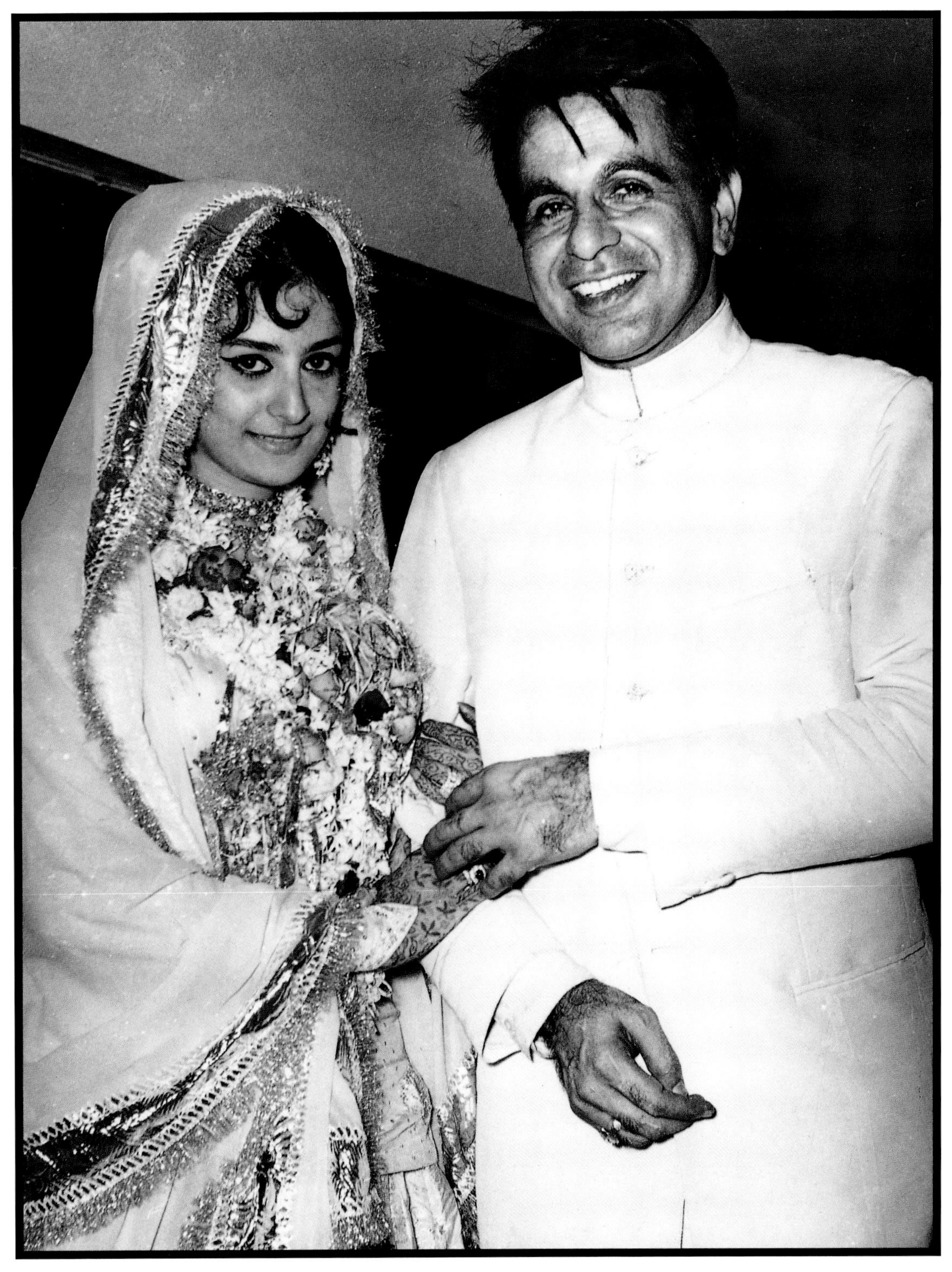

Marriage of Dilip Kumar, film actor, and Saira Banu

Left: Nimmi, film actress

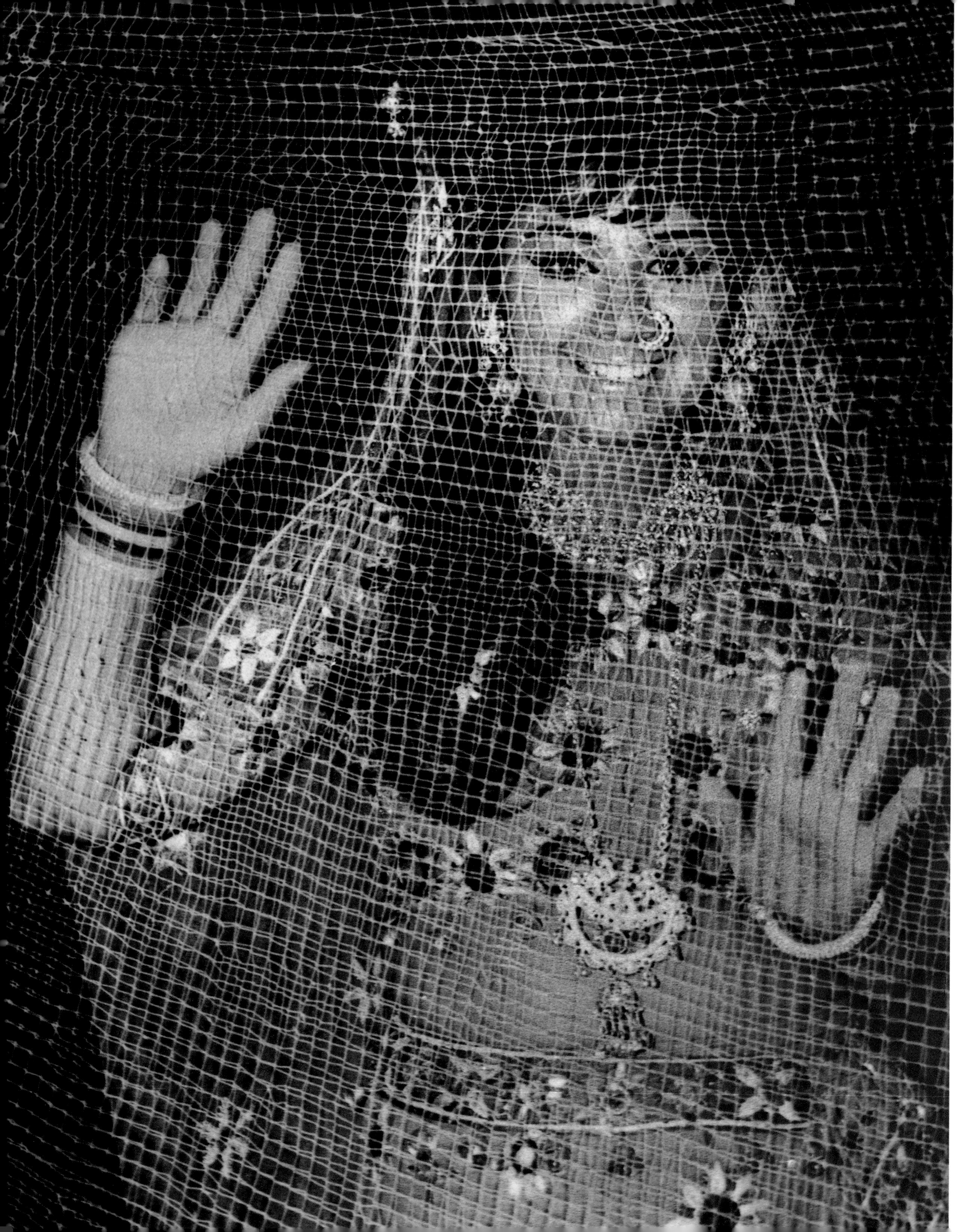

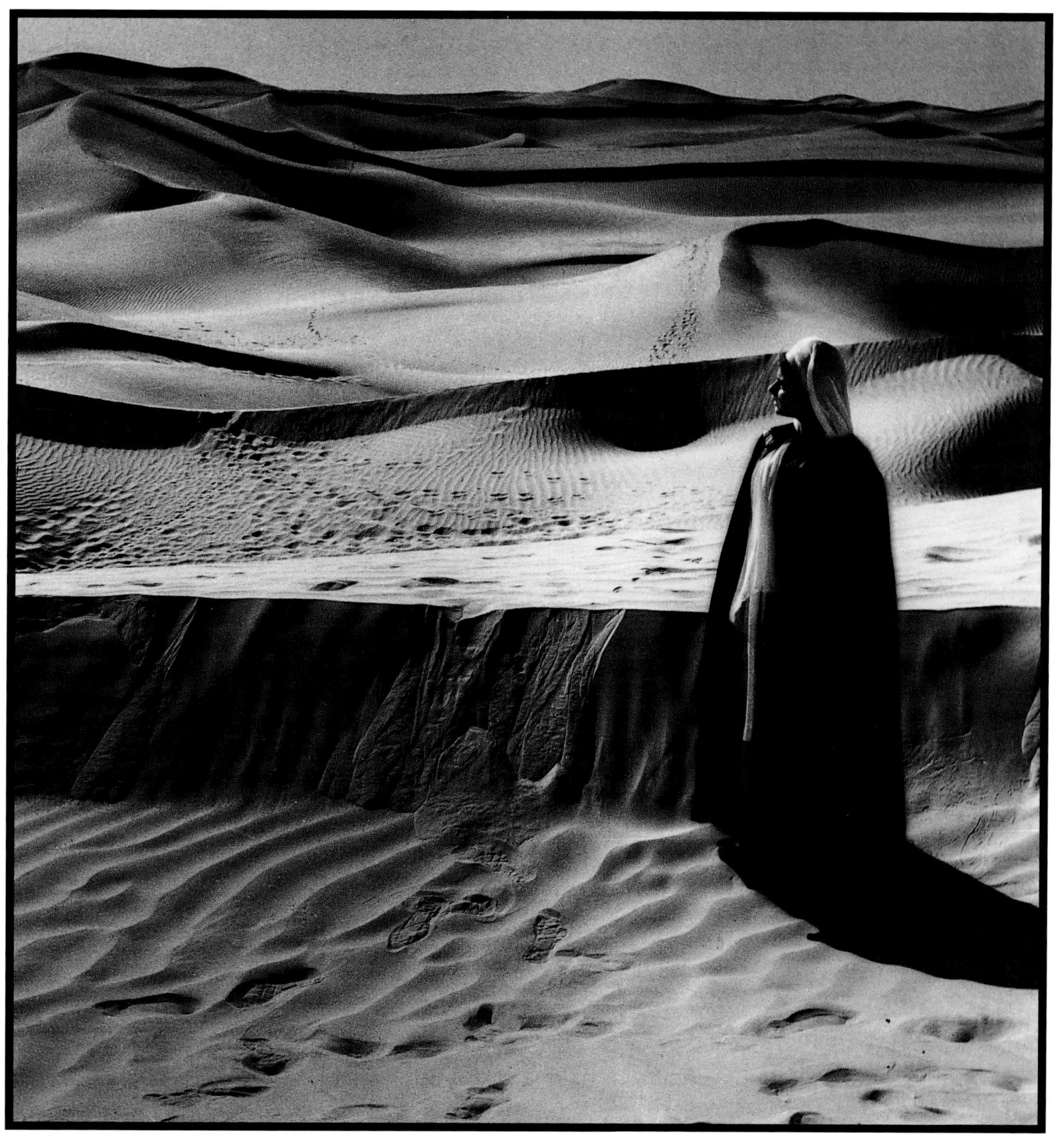

Nazima, film actress

Left: Farida Jalal, film actress

I was first introduced to Mr. A L Syed (Abid Mian to us ever after)
through The World's Best Photographs when I was still a student. It
was not until after Independence that I met the man—a frail,
charming figure with the Rolleicord slung on his shoulder. We
met umpteen times at the photographic meets at Hyderabad,
Bangalore, Calcutta and Delhi. He would always bring a box of
photographs and we would delight in his collection. His technique
was so superb that when others were still fidgeting to focus and
prepare the shot, he had already 'clicked', and what a telling
picture it would be. I was fortunate to have his life-long friendship.
May his soul rest in peace.

P N Mehra
New Delhi

Right: A L Syed and Mr. R D Mathur

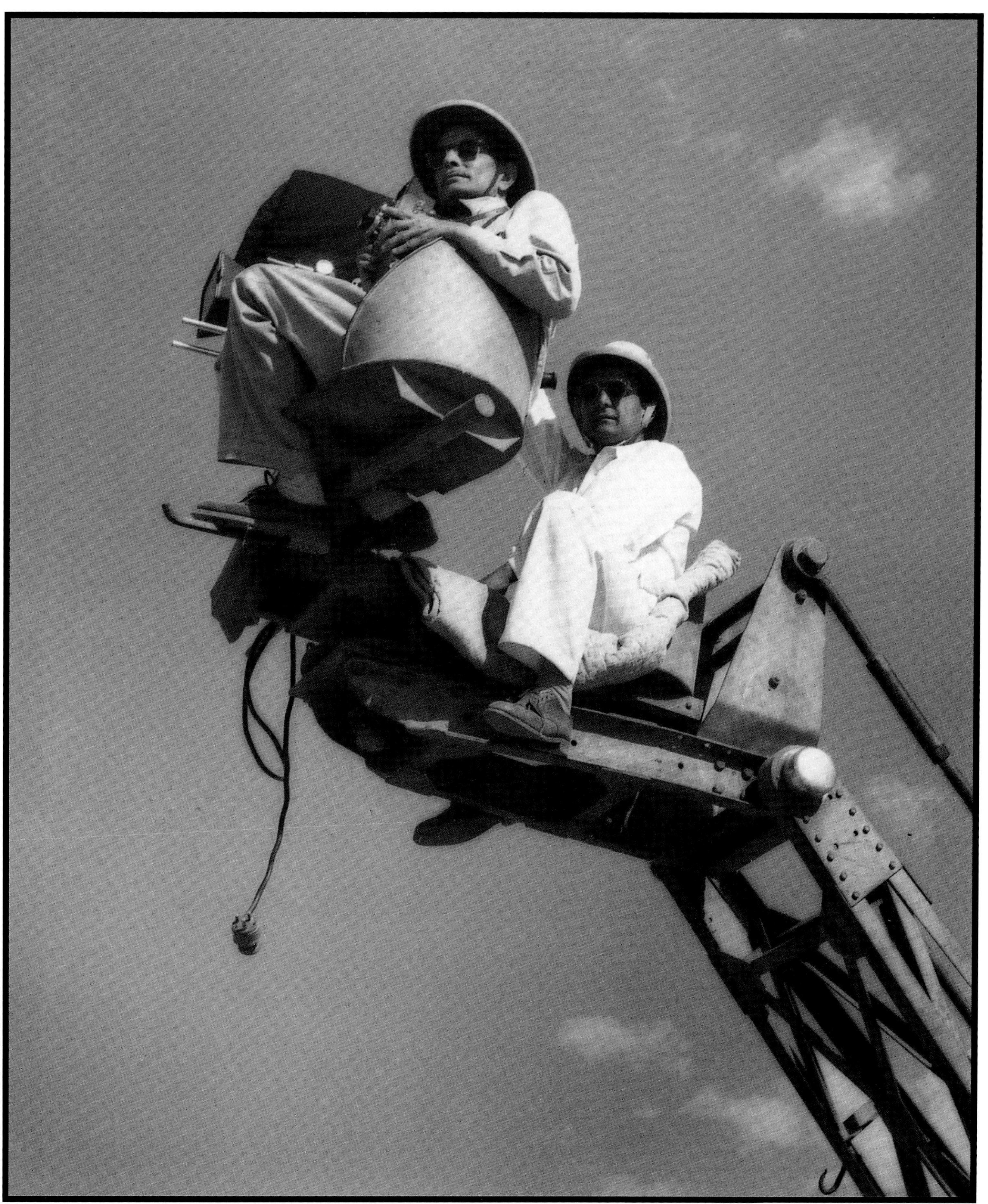

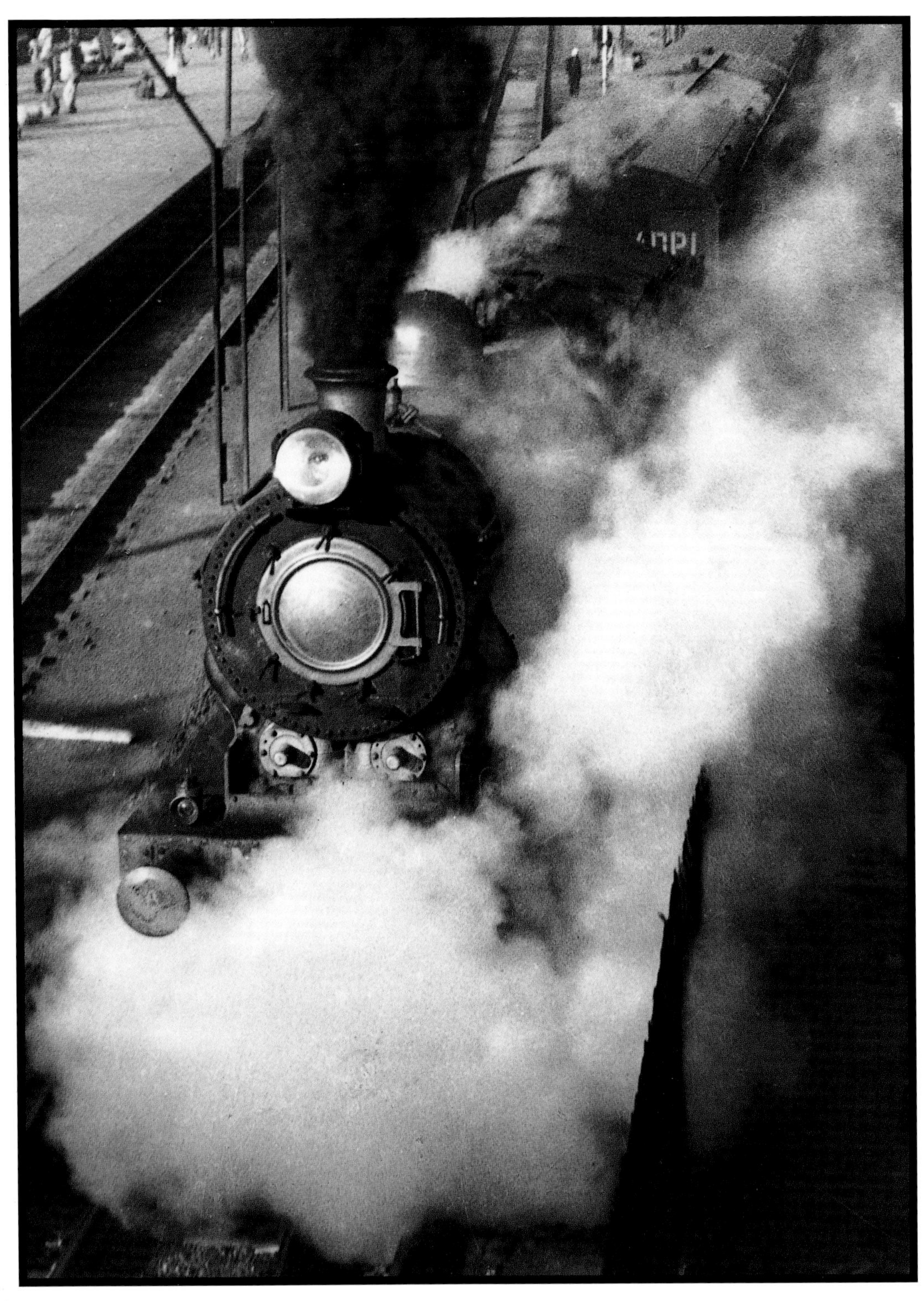

Ready to move, Delhi

Right: Marine Drive, Bombay

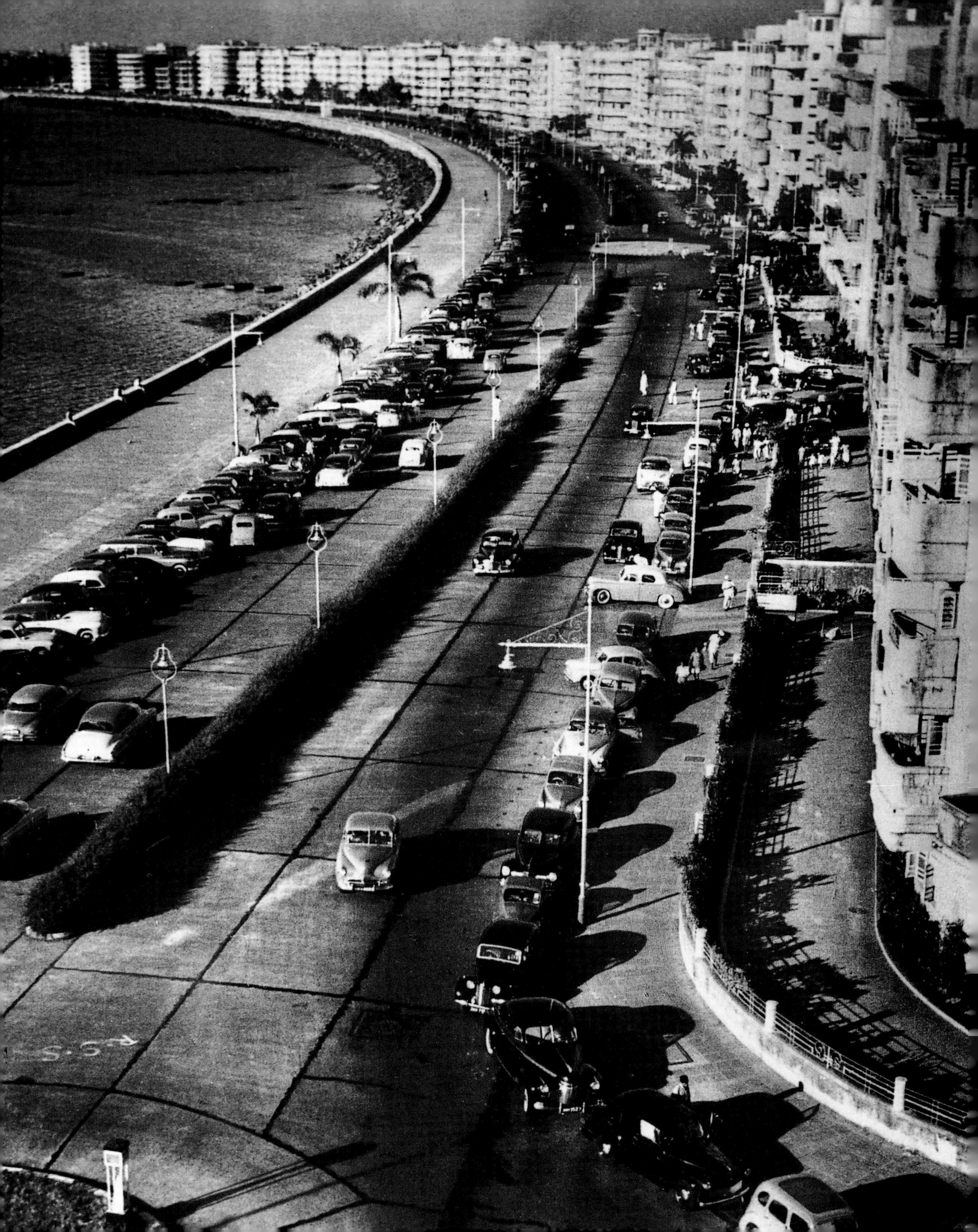

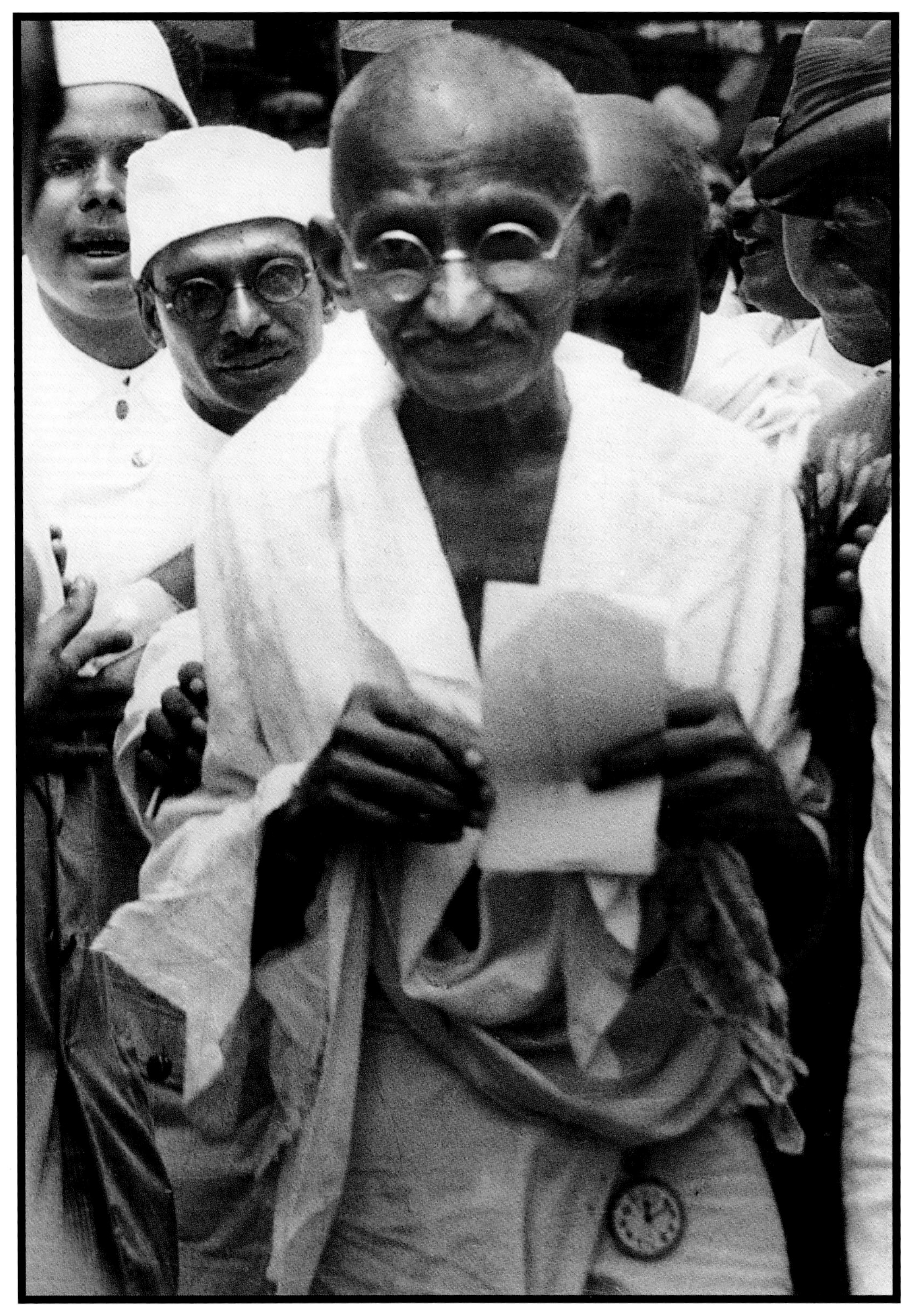

Gandhiji, Round Table Conference, London, 1936

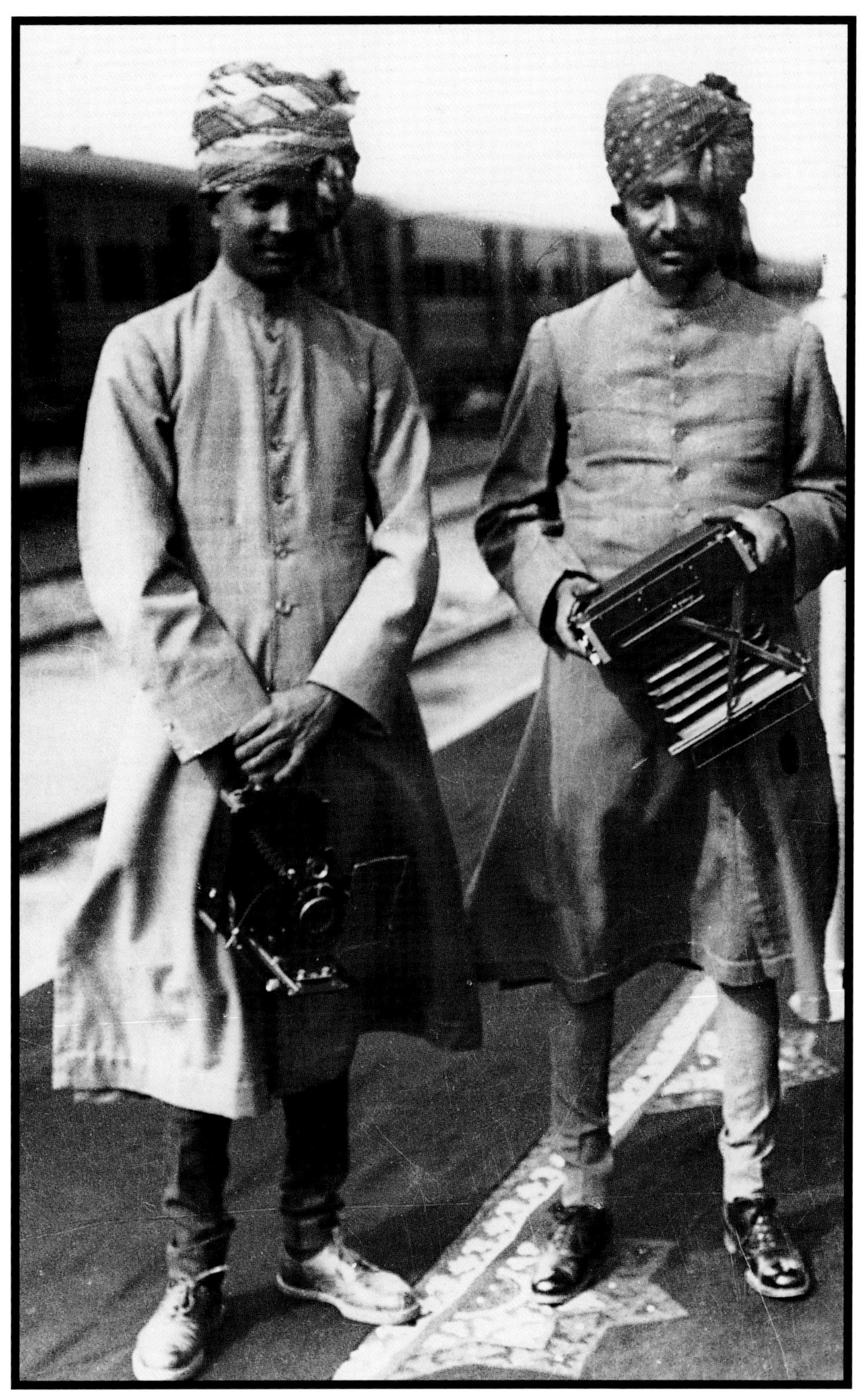

A L Syed and K L Syed, Bikaner, 1925

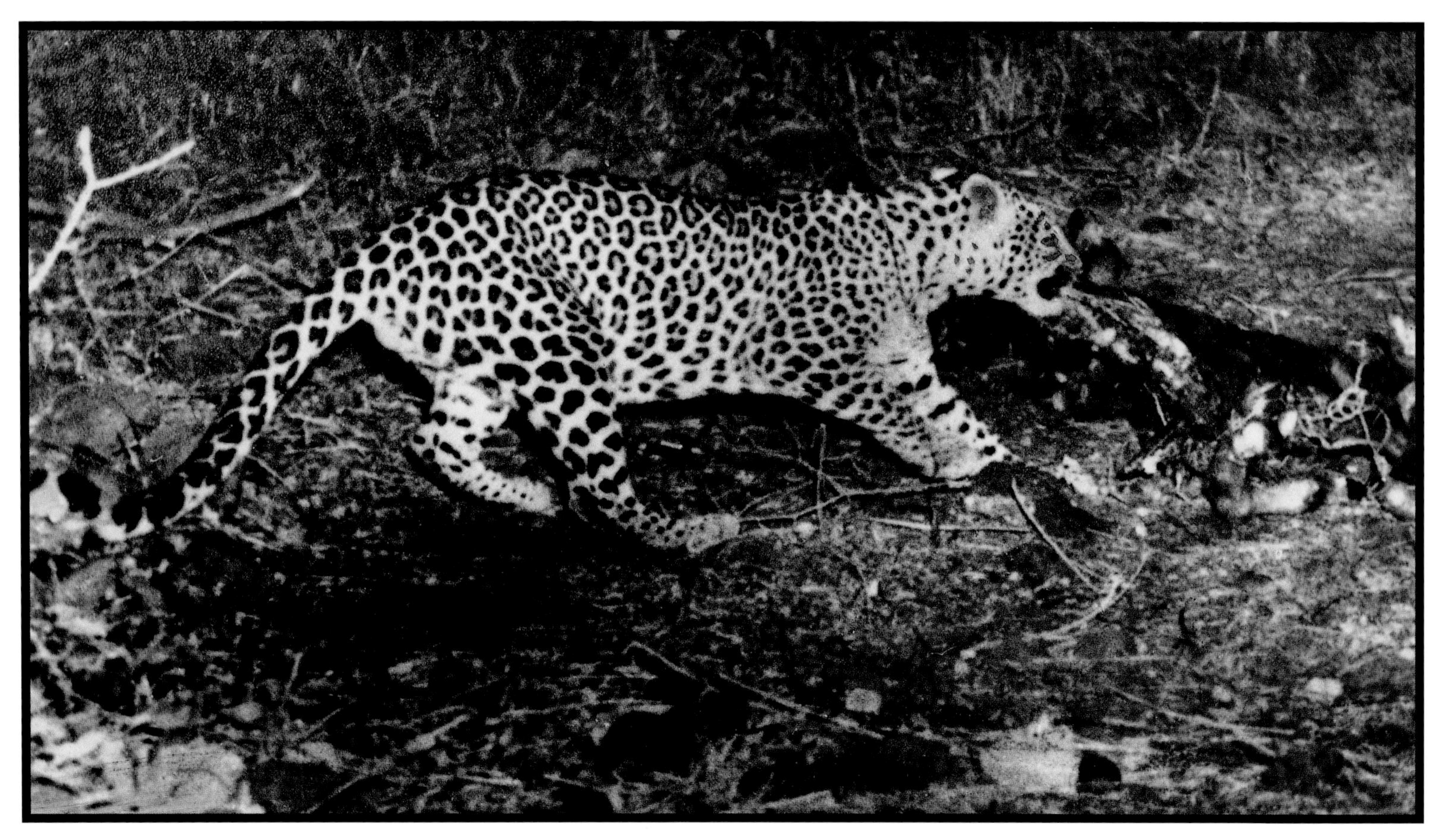

Leopard dragging the kill, Kishangarh, Rajasthan

Right: King of the forest, Gwalior

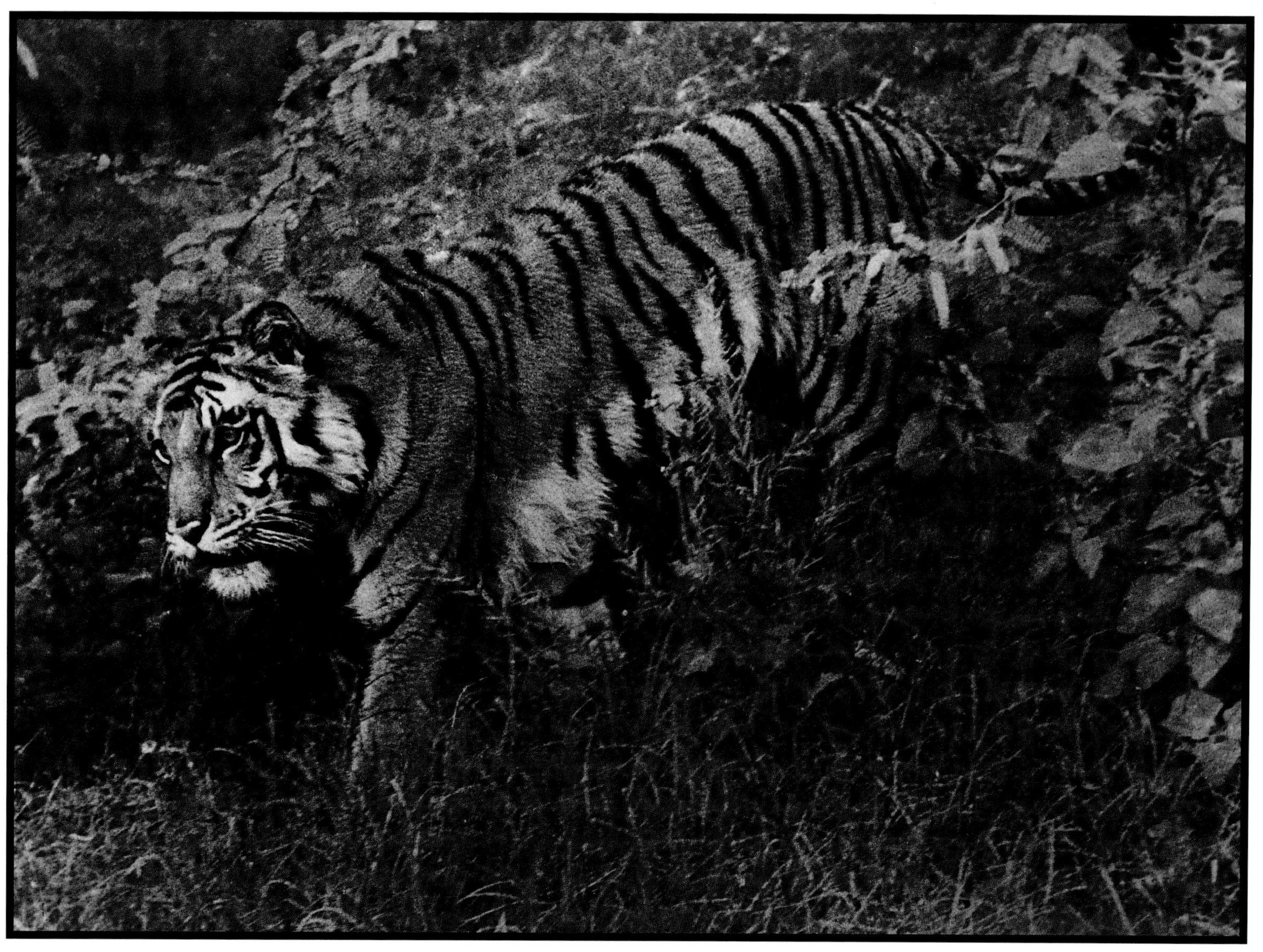

Mr. A L Syed was my uncle as well as my father-in-law. Having enjoyed this dual relationship, I had an opportunity to be in his vicinity and observe him very closely.

He had two prominent interests: photography and hunting. He was very quick in capturing the rare moments of life on celluloid. And equally sharp was he in aiming for wild game. While doing outdoor photography in the forest, on one shoulder you would find his rifle and on the other a Rolleicord, both eagerly awaiting their respective chances. On one occasion, while hunting in the dense forest of Madhya Pradesh he came face to face with a tiger. His obsession for getting big game was sparked and he put his finger on the trigger. Immediately his heart cried out, what a beautiful animal! In a fraction of a second he changed his mind, and instead of firing a shot he captured the animal's image through the eye of his camera. From that moment photography became his first love.

Sabbir K Syed
Syed Photographers, Palanpur

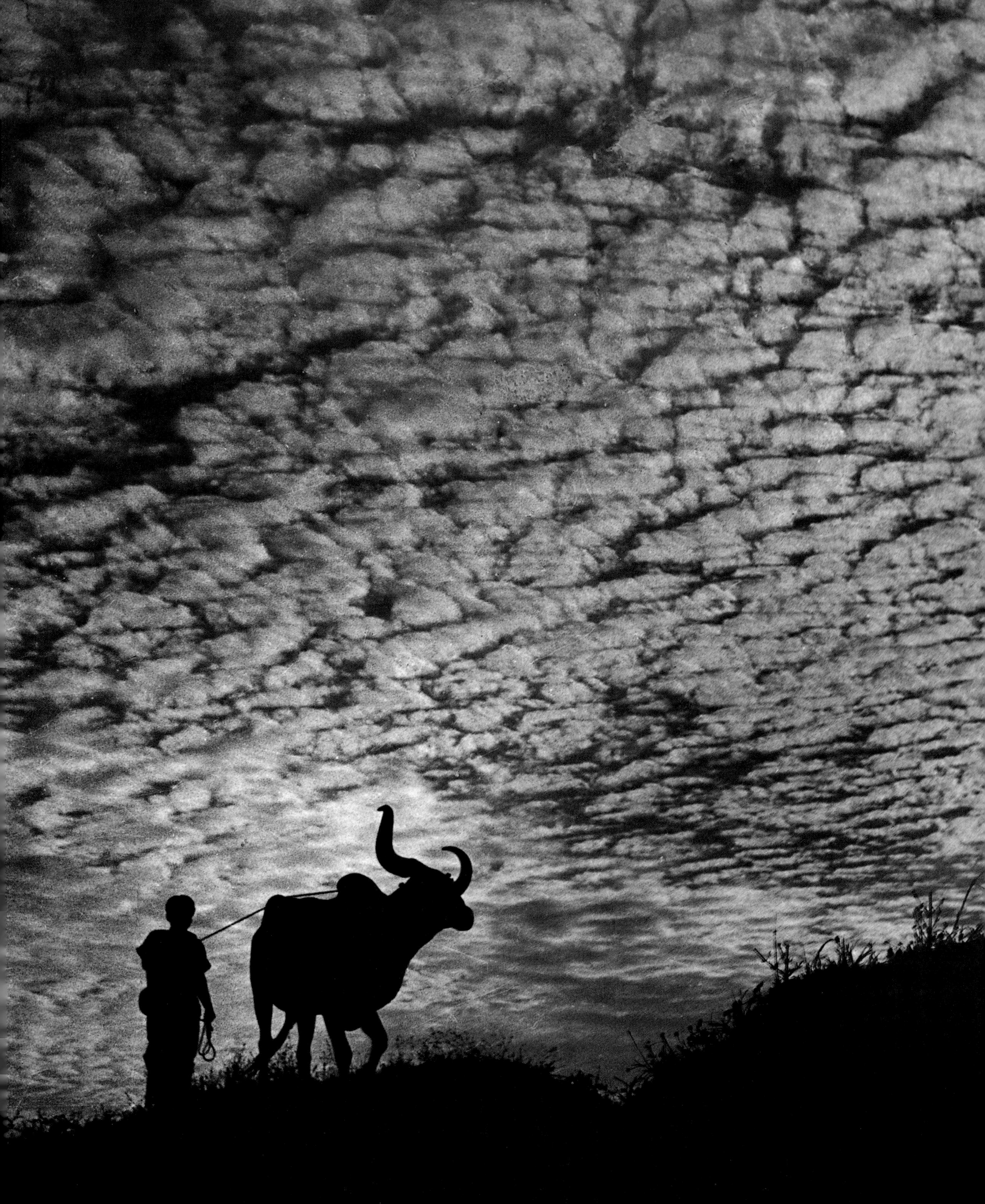

My first meeting with Janab A L Syed in 1955 in Shimla was an
enlightening experience. He was the most famous photographer in
India, yet his humbleness was his most striking quality. On
subsequent meetings I found him warm, considerate, helpful and
bestowed with a very sharp memory. He will live in the memory of
all those who came into contact with him even remotely. I
personally rate him as the photographer of the century and a man
of all times.

B S Sodhi
Ambala

Left: At dusk, Gujarat

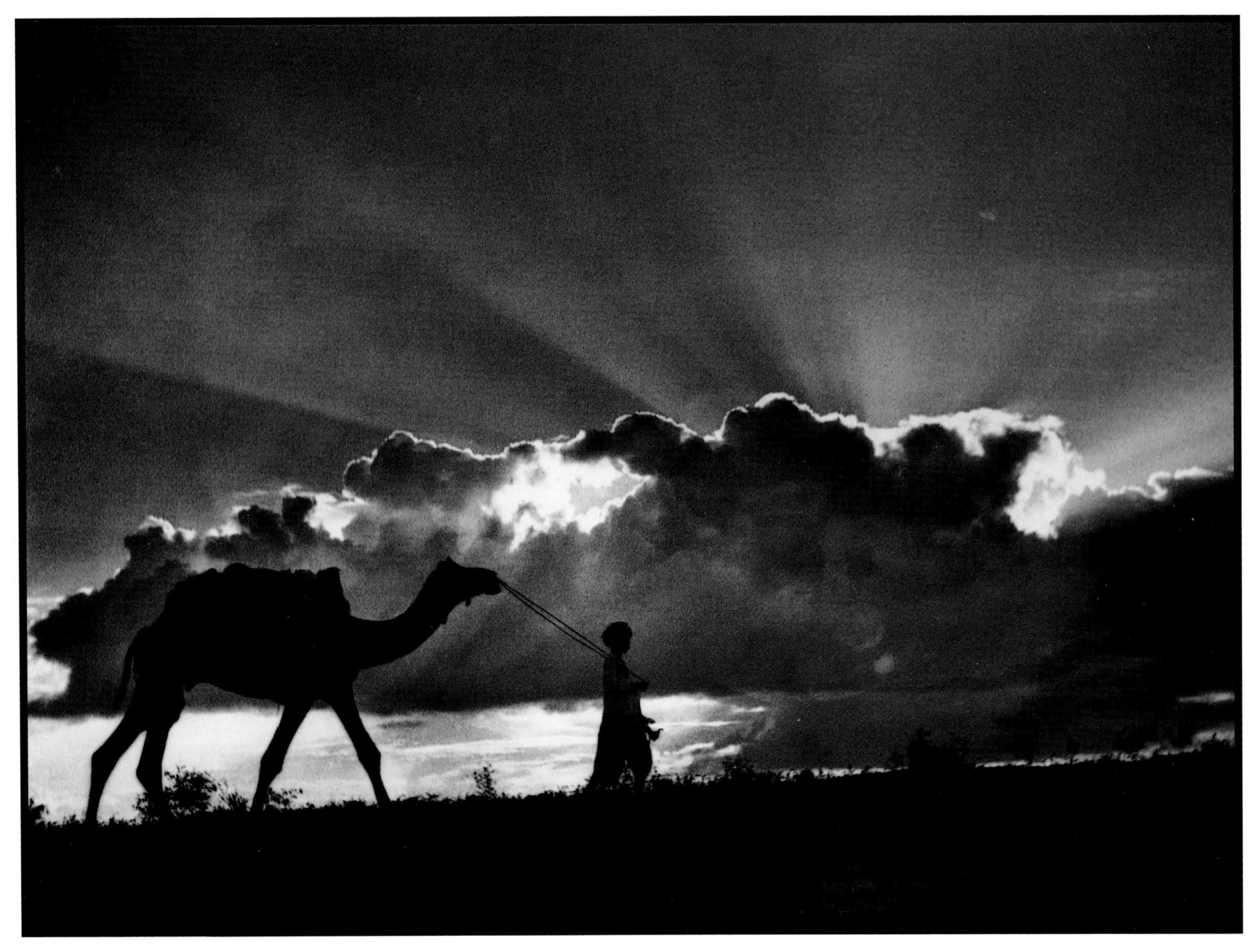

Traveller of the East, Palanpur (*Popular Photography* award winner, 1935)

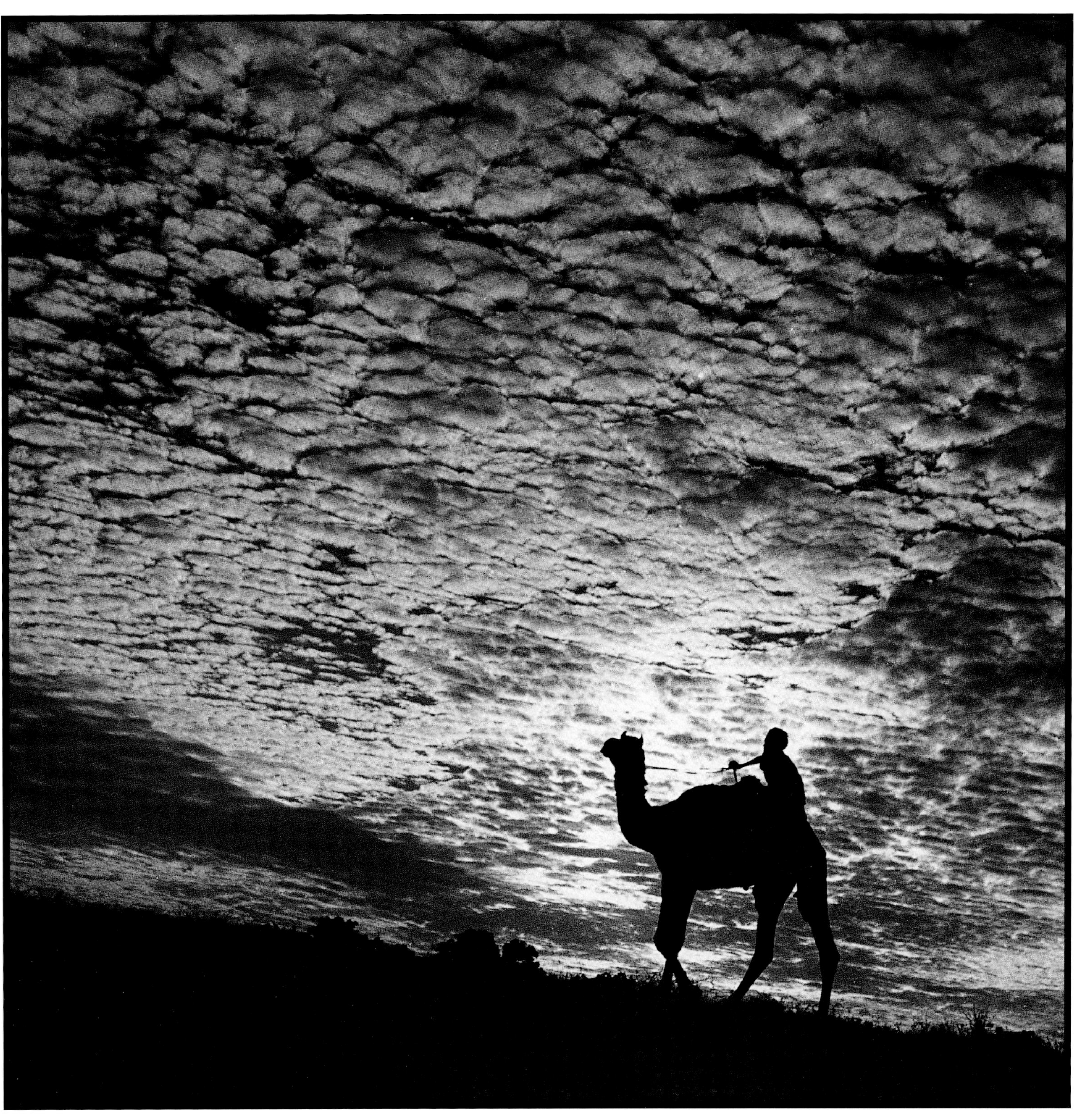

Back to home, near Palanpur

We first met Syed sahib in 1964 and from 1970 till he passed away, we were among those fortunate to have been in constant touch with him.

We pay our humble tribute to him for the joy that he brought to us through his great company and through the letters he wrote to us in his own handwriting, which must have been very trying for him because he suffered from Parkinson's disease. He once wrote one of his own couplets in Urdu to describe his physical problems and how helpless he felt:

A person who has been a success all his life,
how could he ever imagine that one day, due to old age
he would be helpless and unable to carry out his work
which was the very life of him?

We shall cherish these letters, full of affection and advice, from the kindest soul who unhesitatingly sharing his vast knowledge. He was a father figure to all of us.

Chitrangada Sharma and O P Sharma
New Delhi

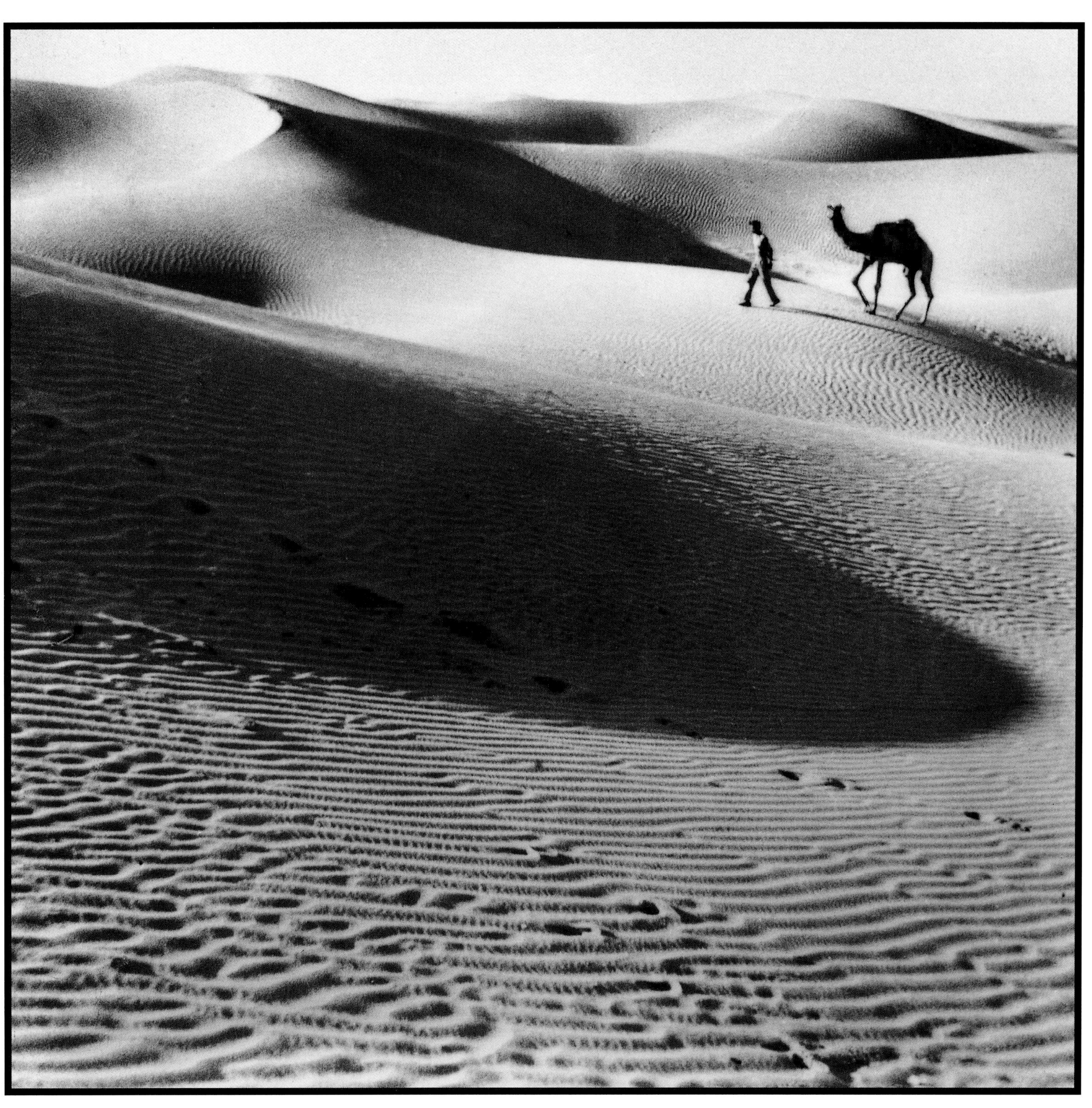

Miles to go, Rajasthan

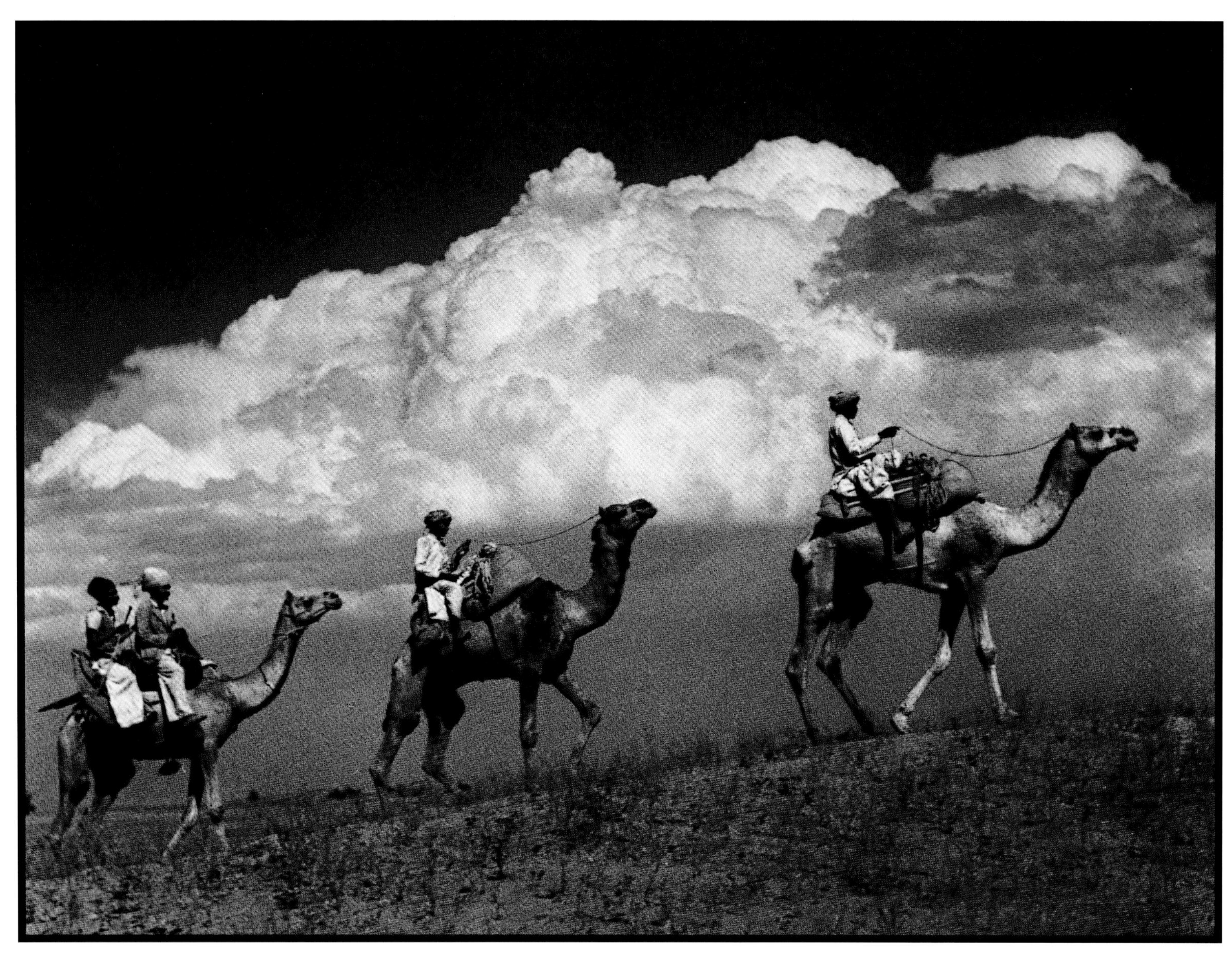

Monsoon evening, Palanpur

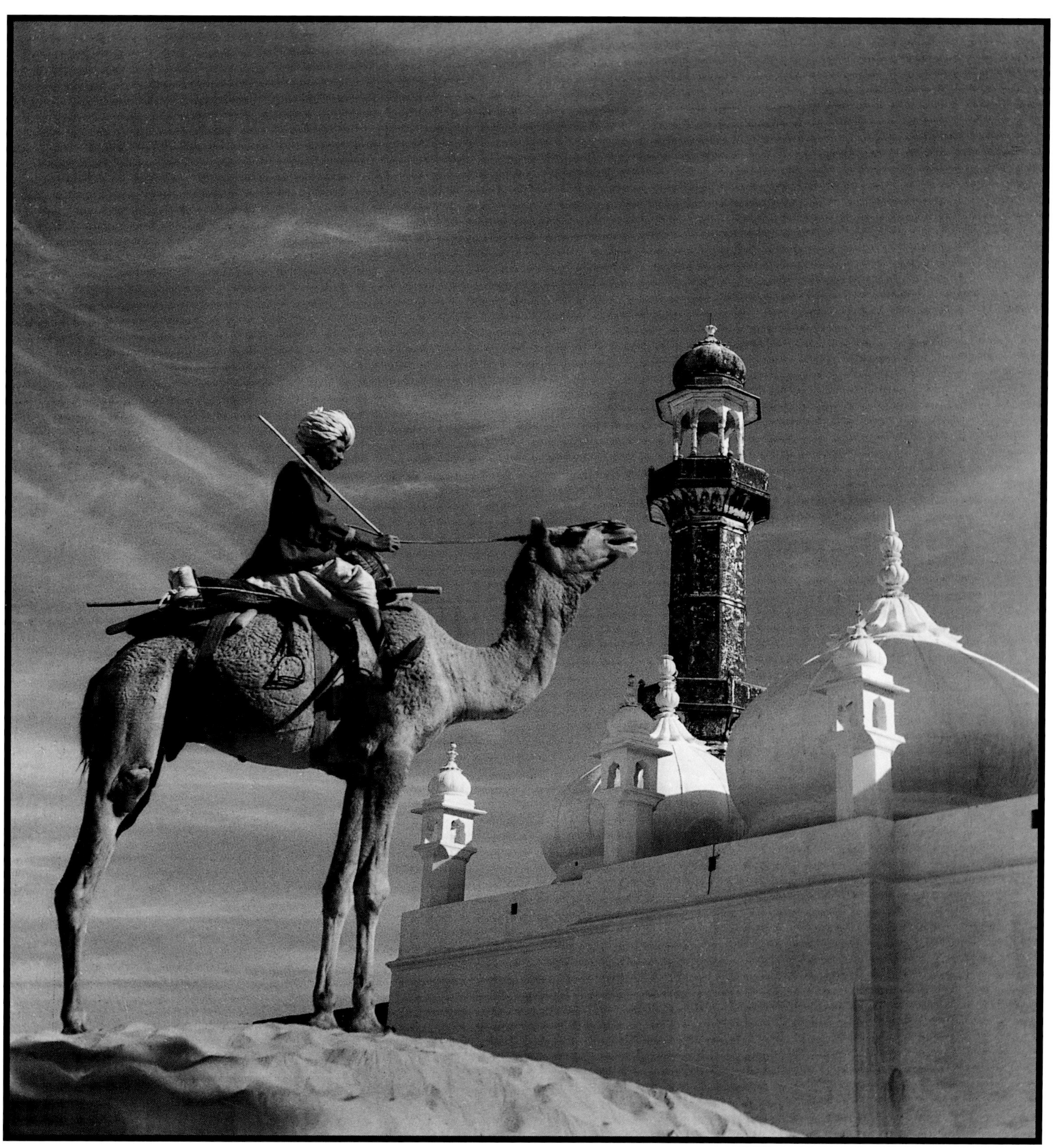

Rest for a while

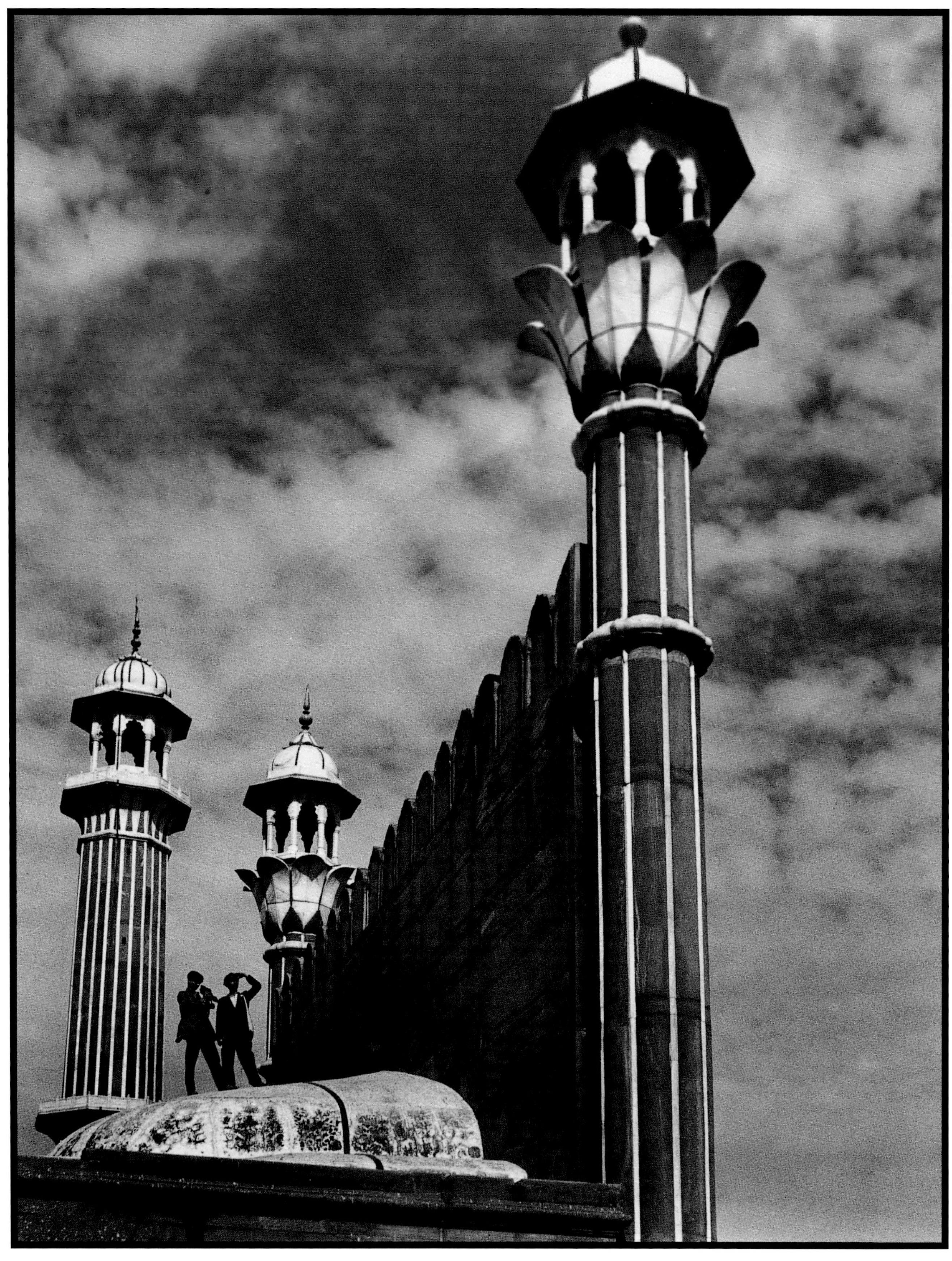

Jama Masjid, Delhi

Right: Jantar Mantar observatory, Jaipur

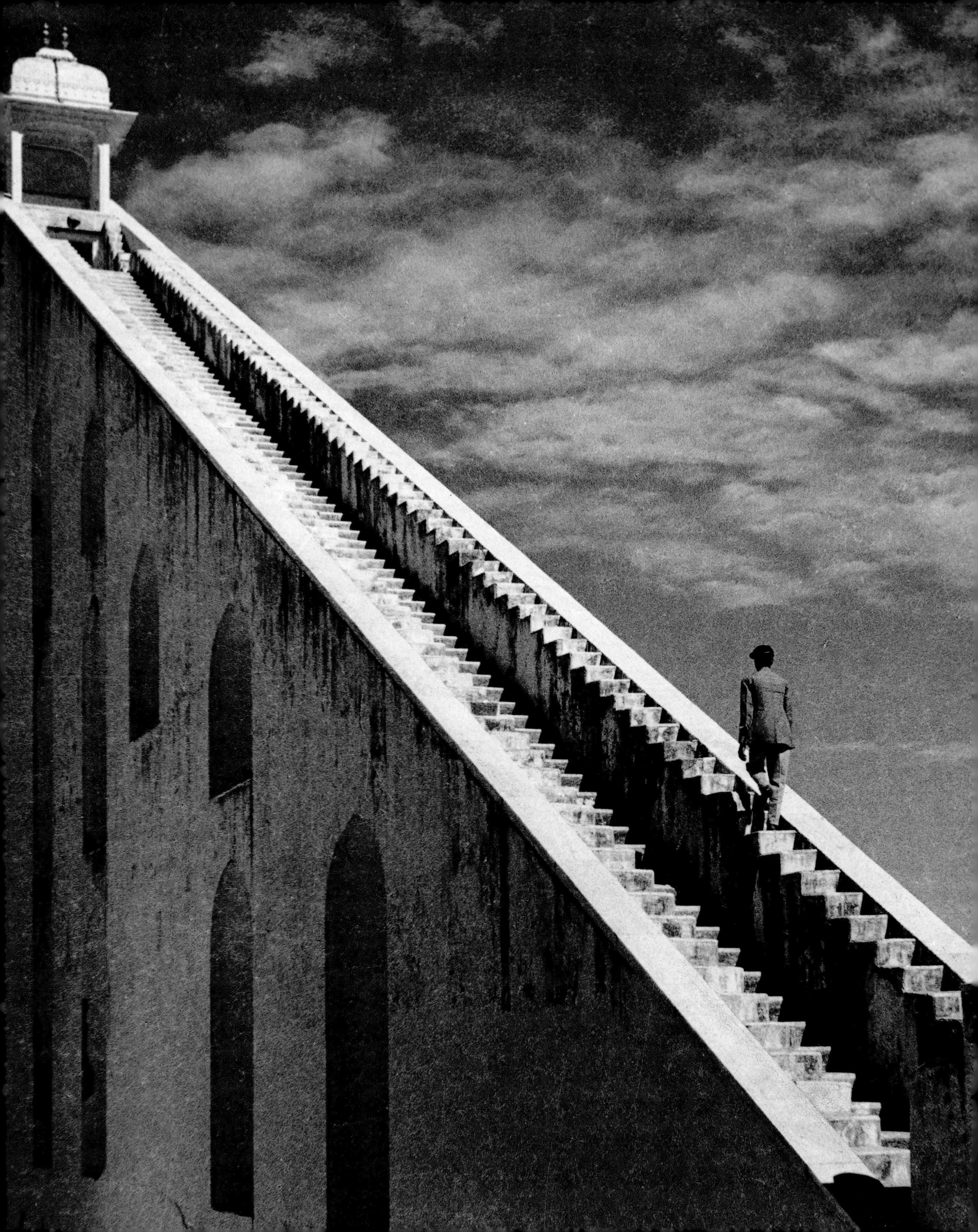

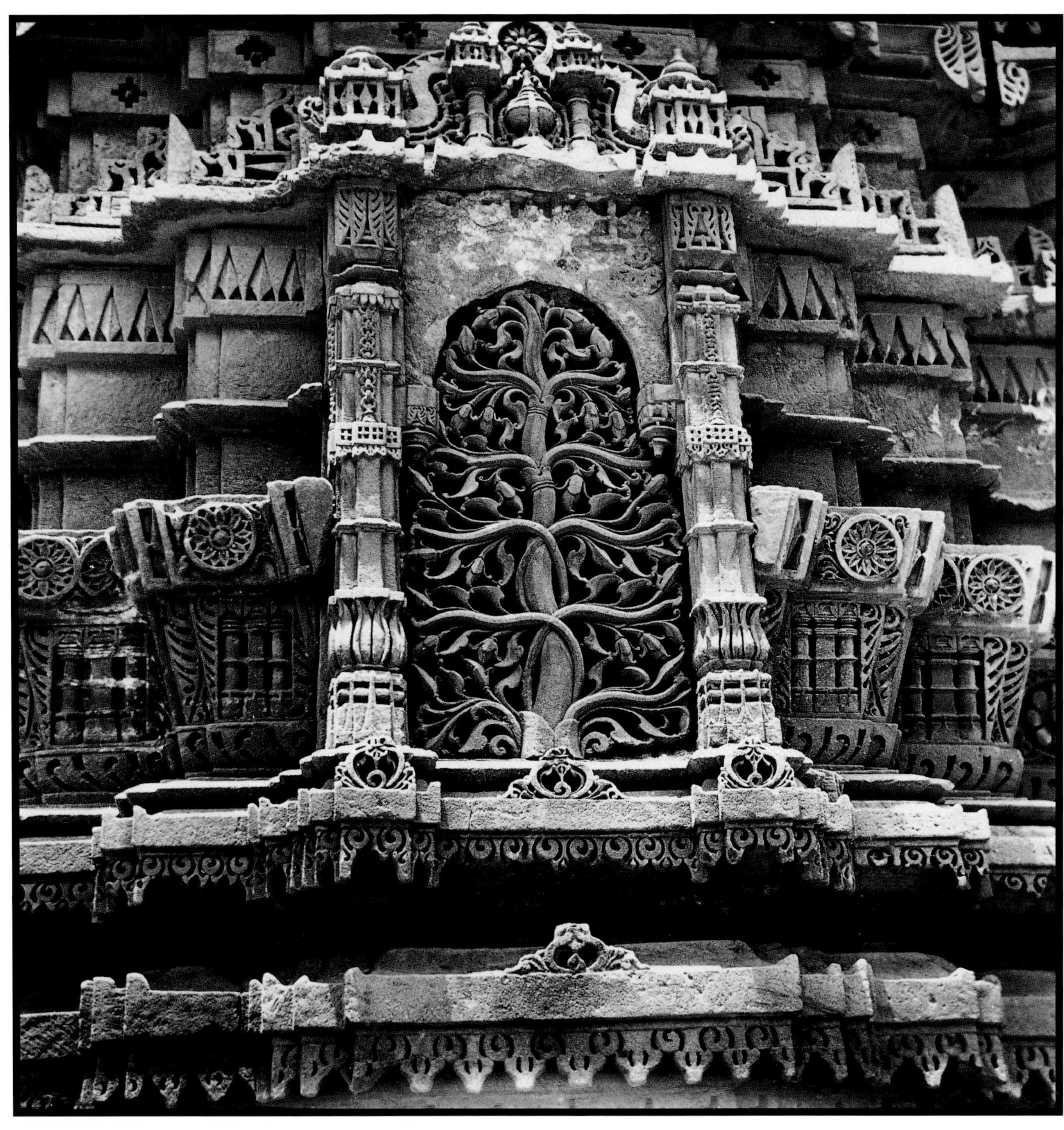

Art in stone

Right: The Temple, Calcutta

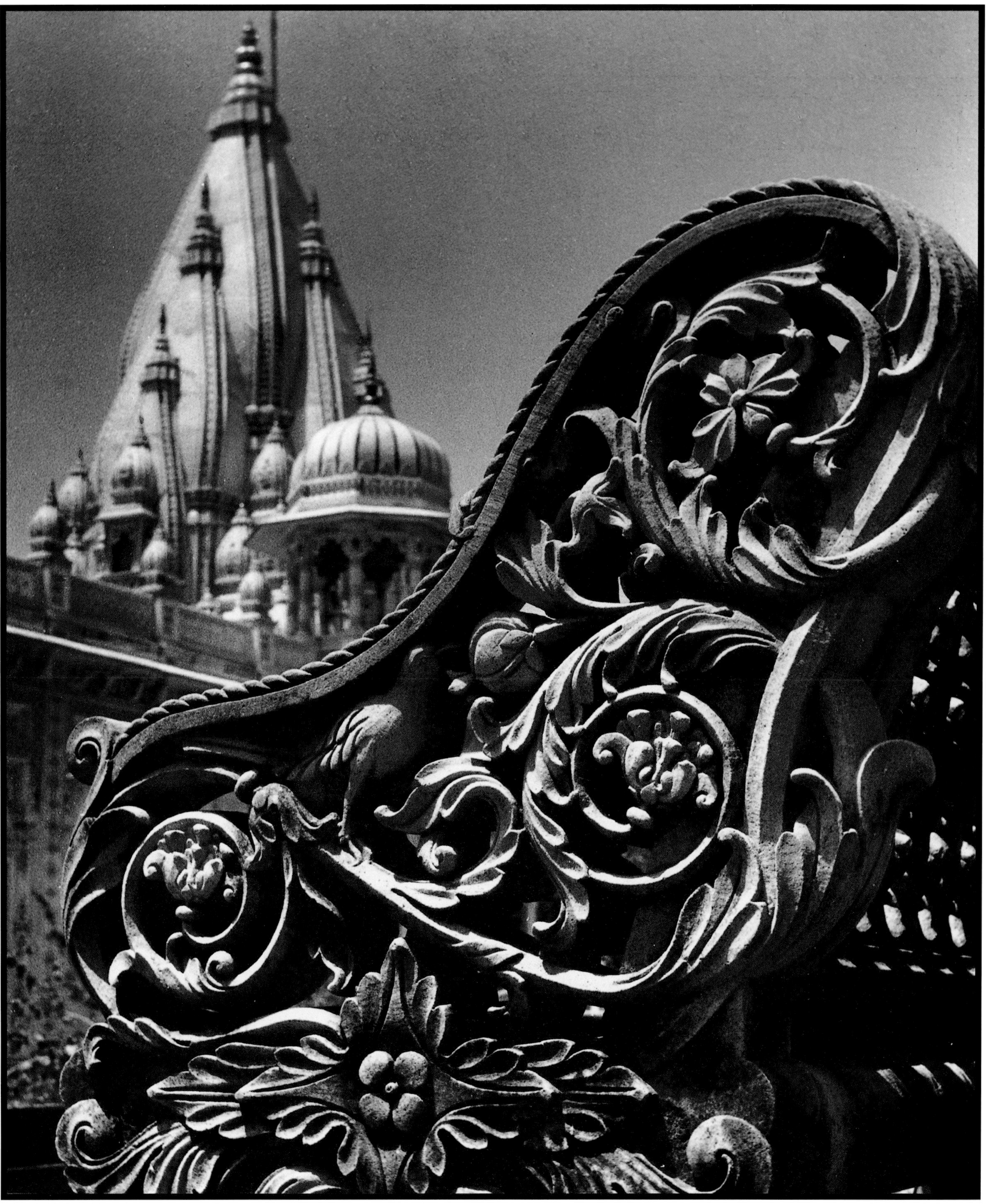

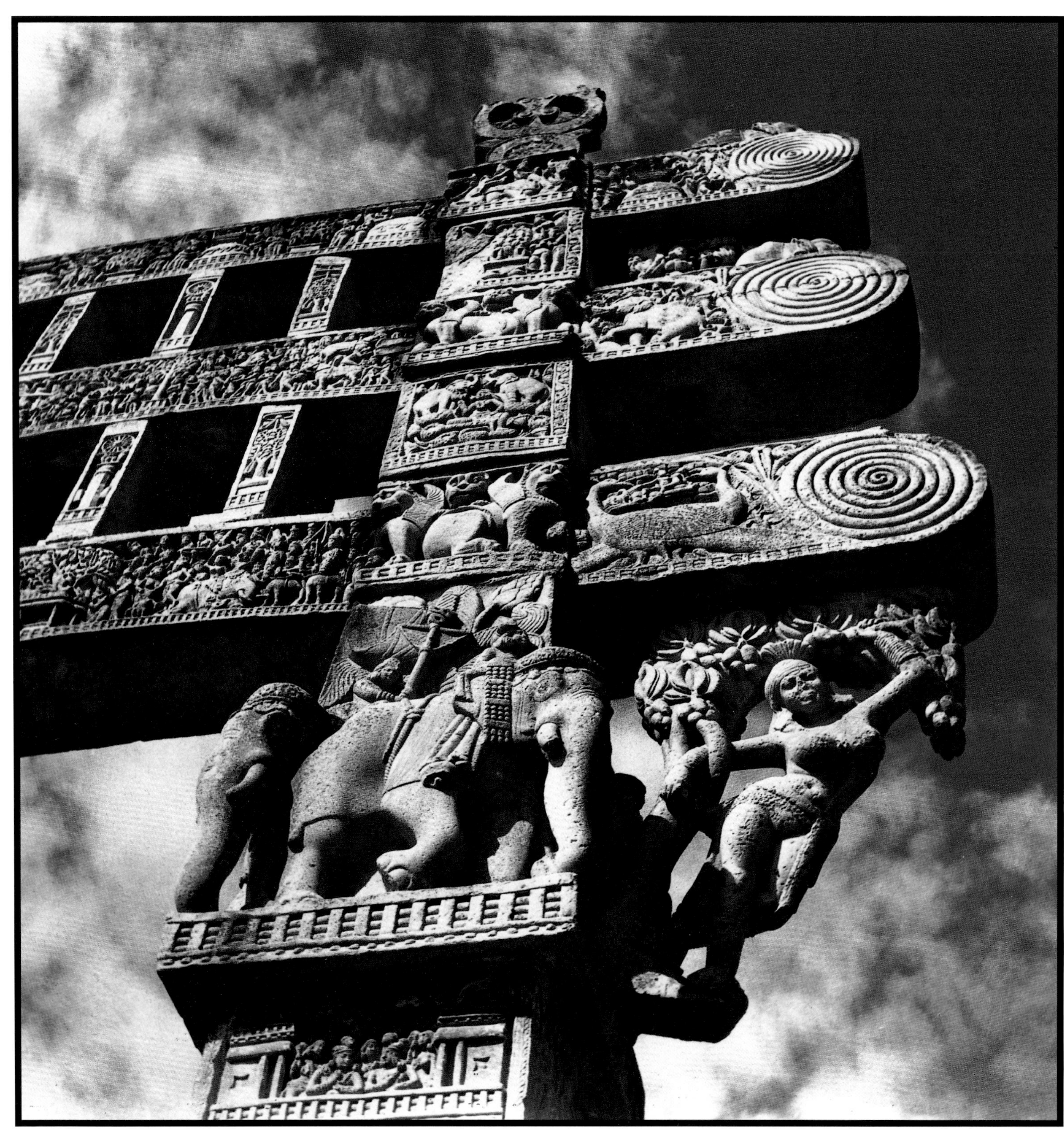

Gateway, Sanchi

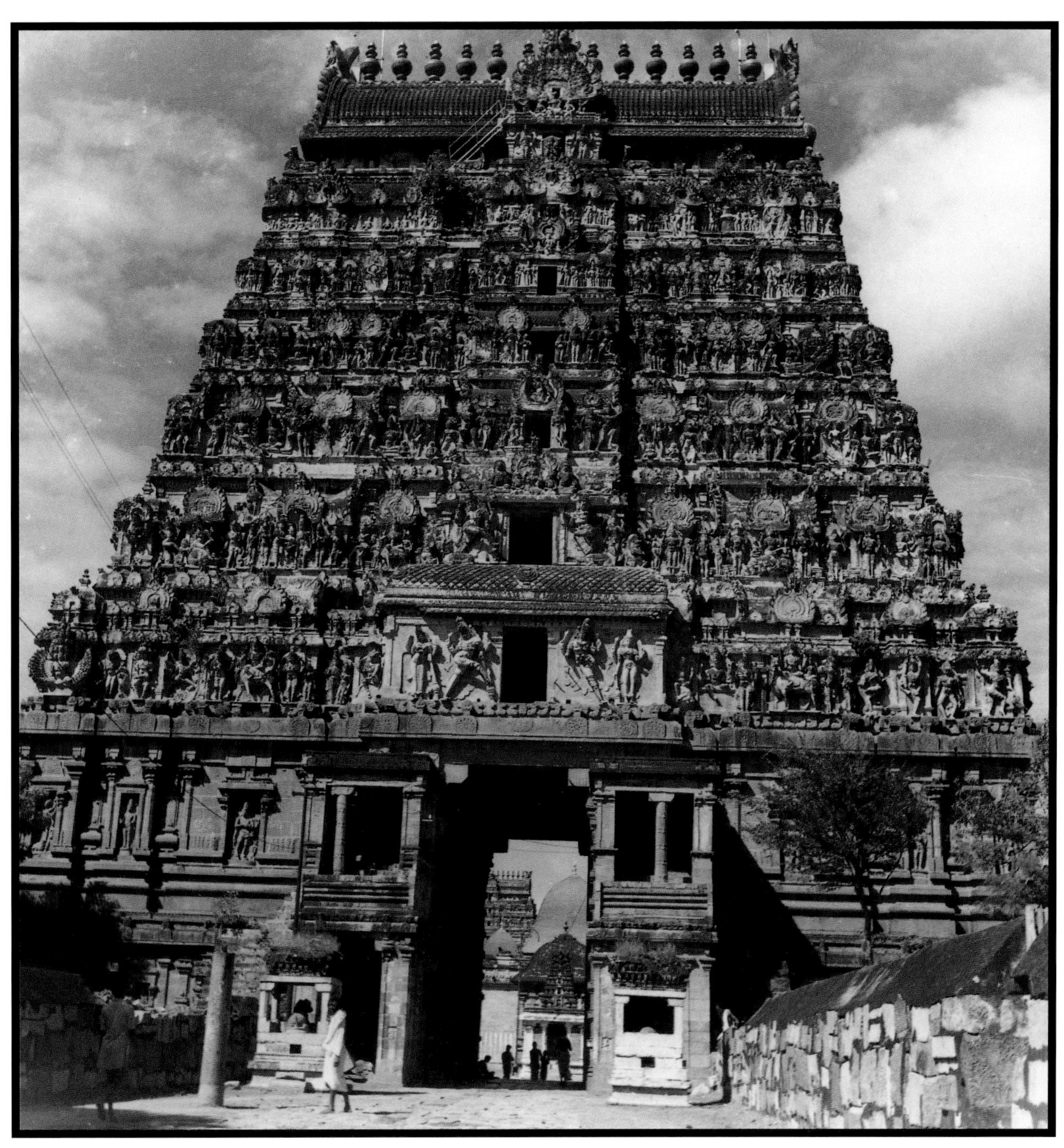

South side of the Kanchipuram temple, Tamilnadu

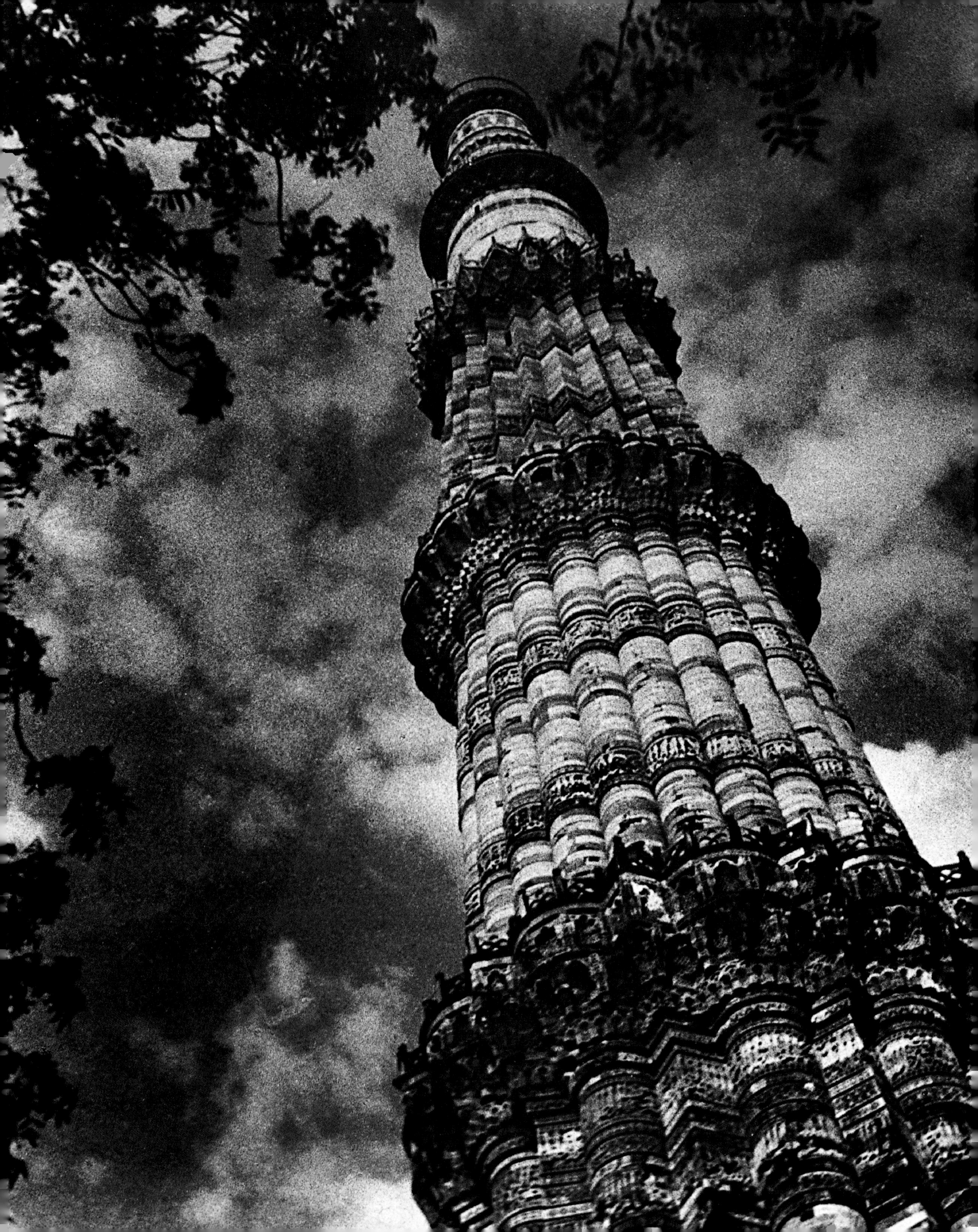

The palace

Left: Kutub Minar, Delhi (Box Camera picture, 1930)

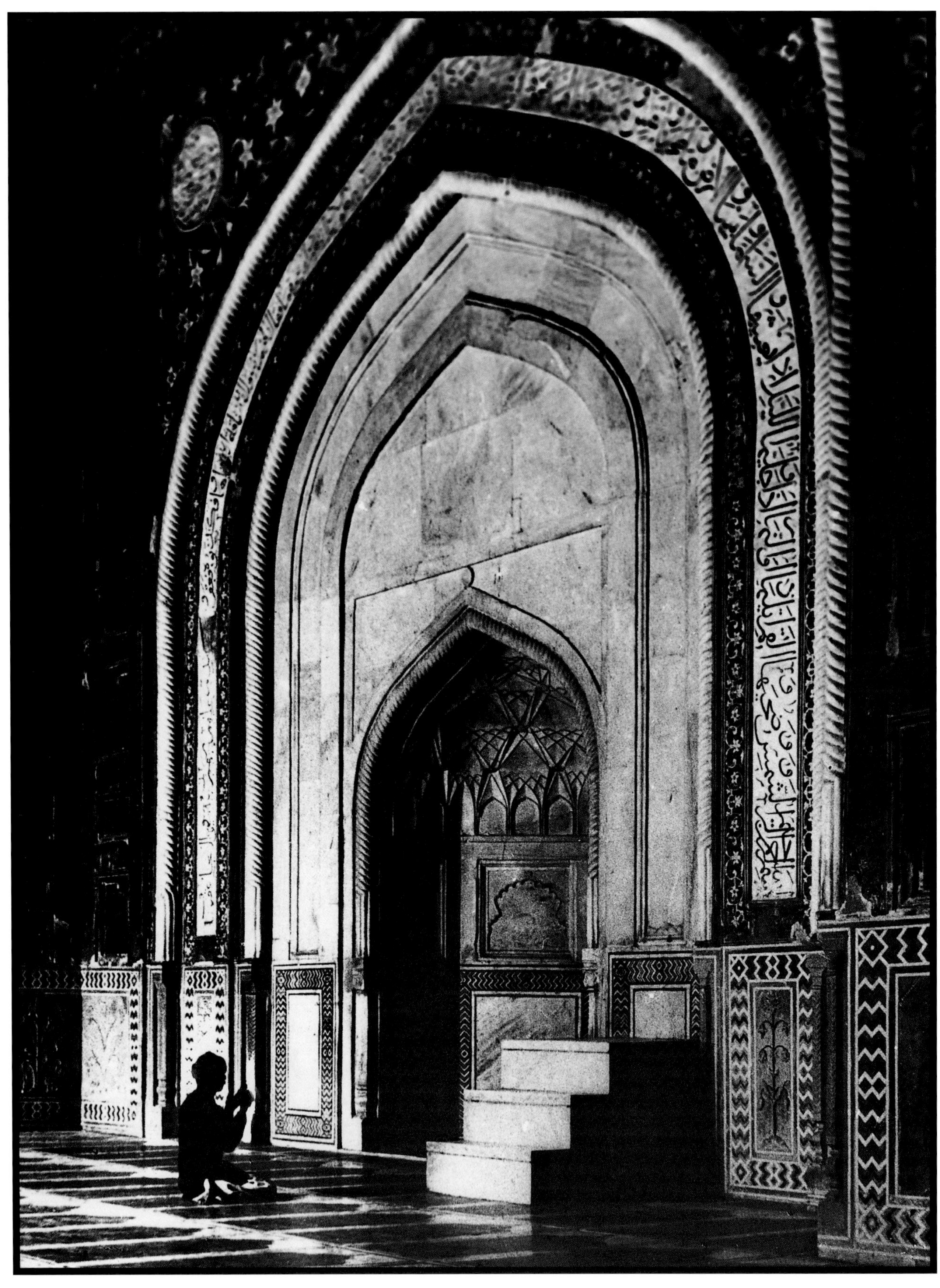

Prayer time, Agra

Right: Bibi Ka Makbura, Aurangabad

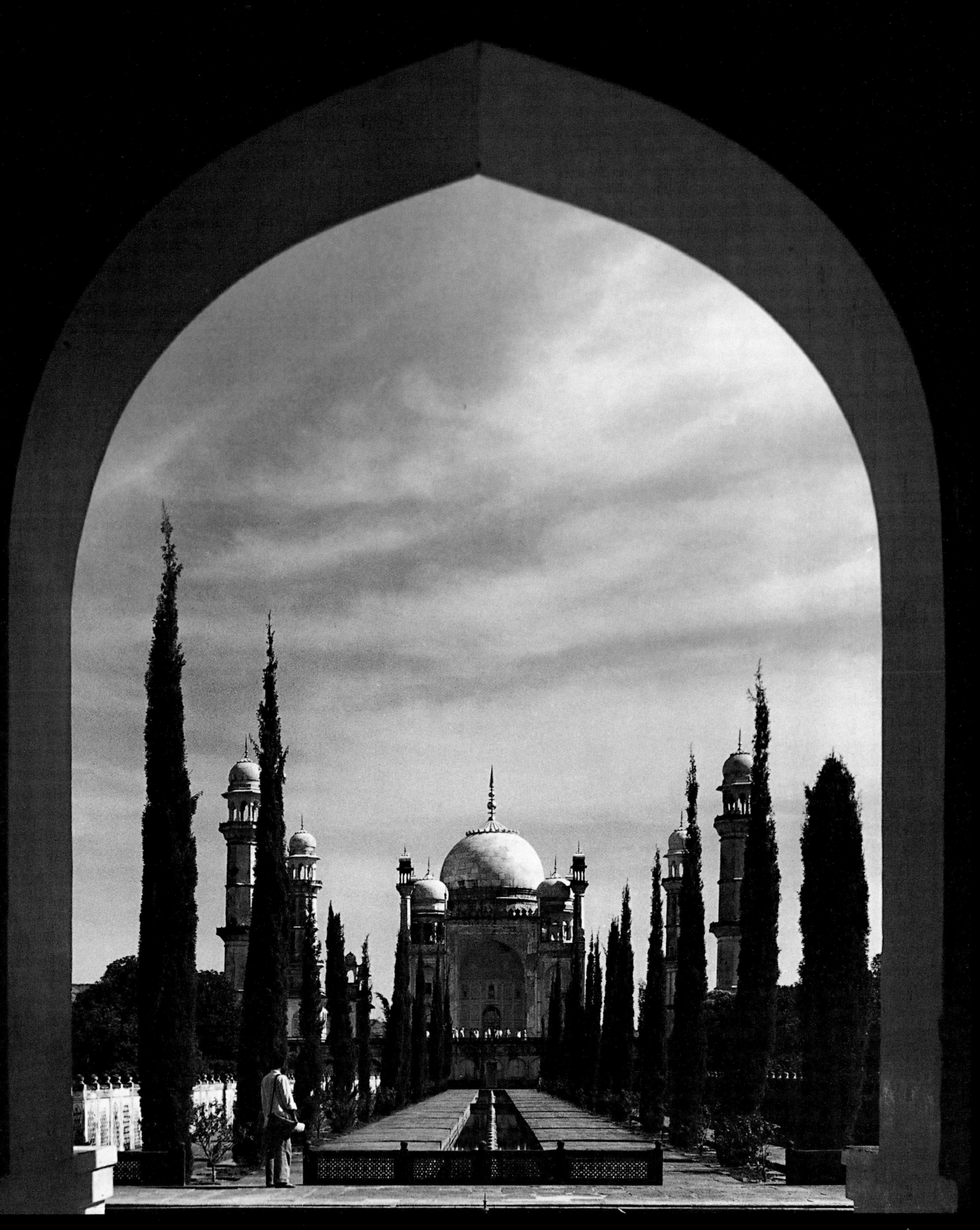

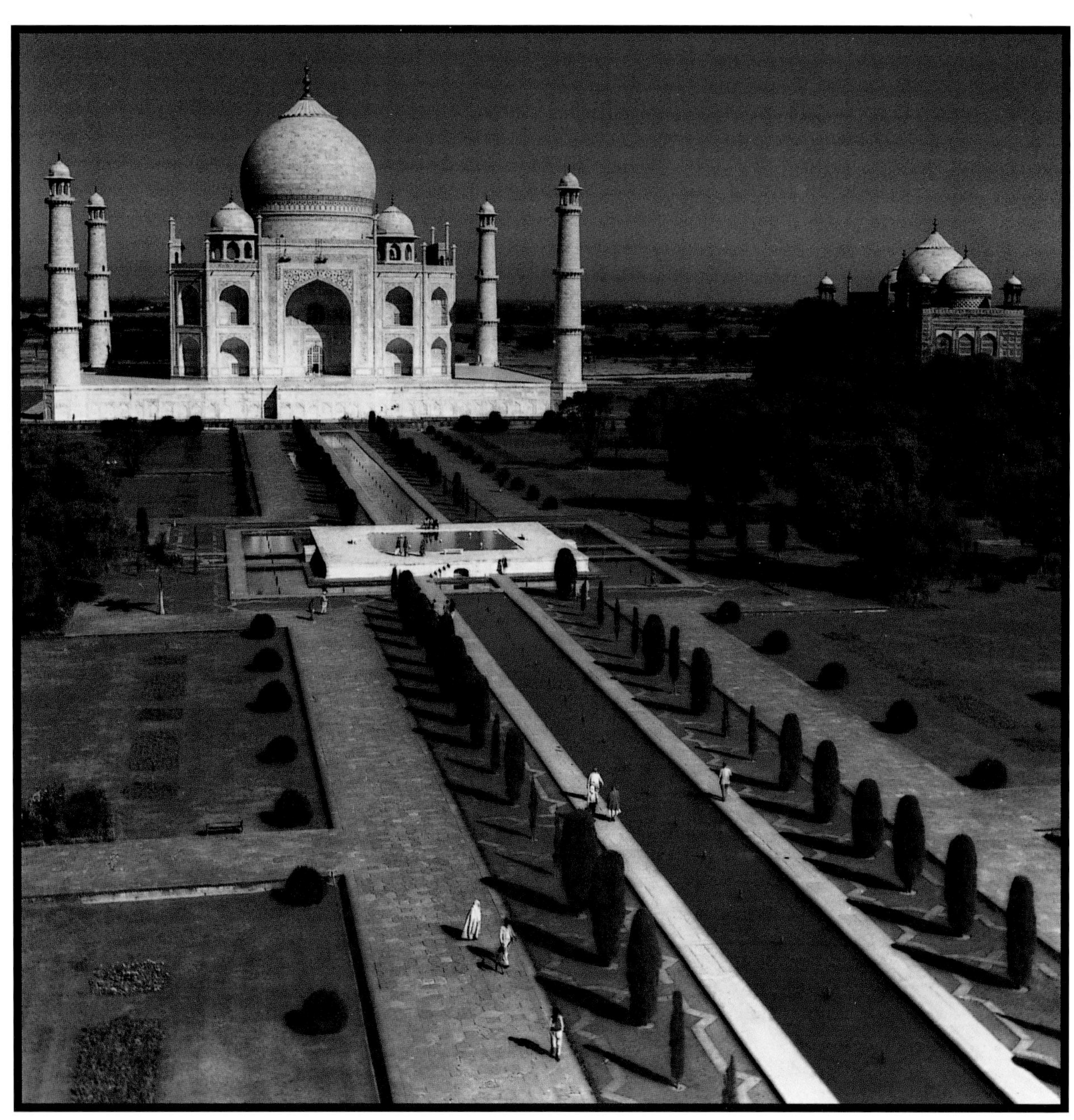

The Taj Mahal, Agra

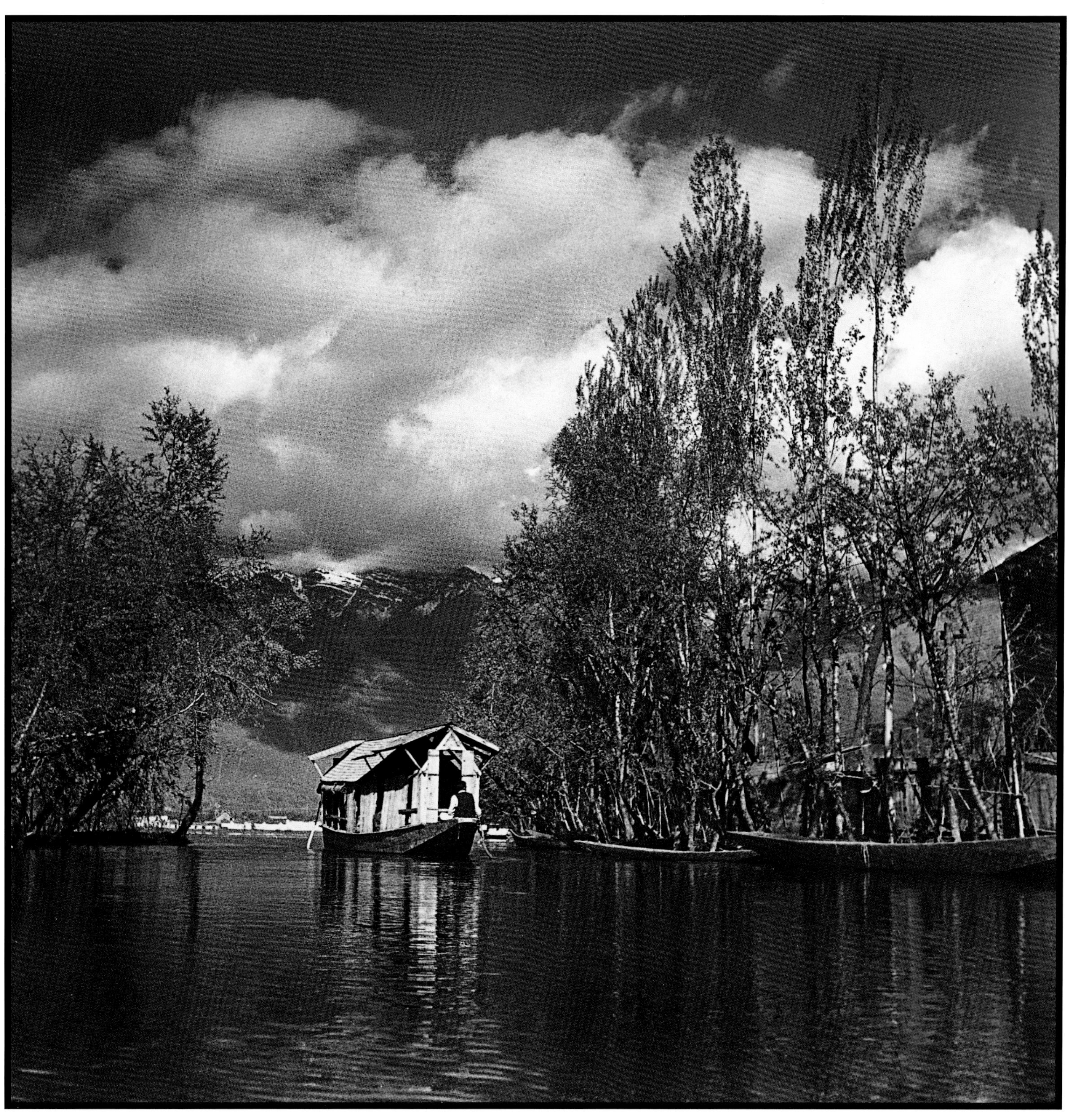

Lone houseboat, Kashmir

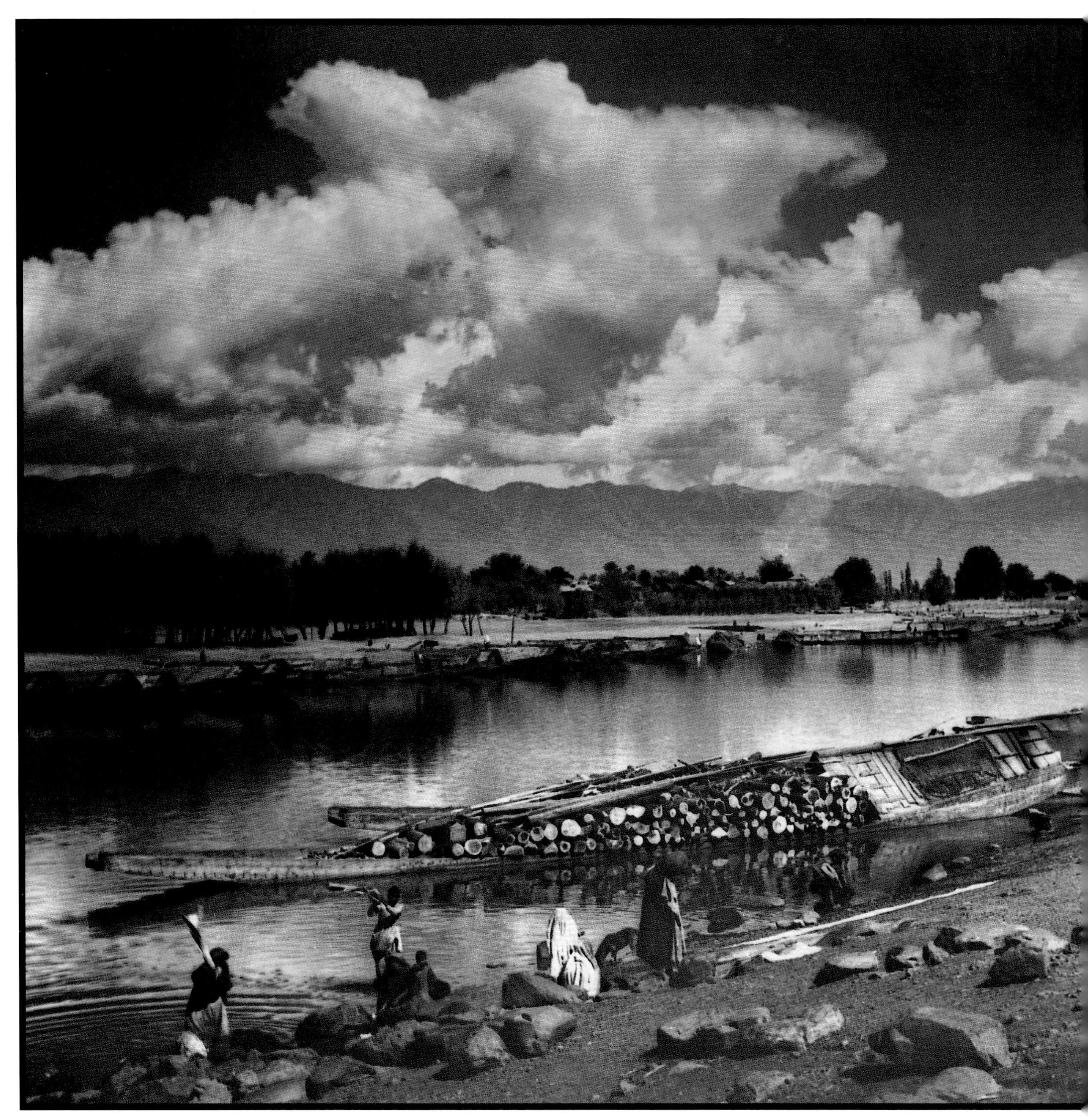

Morning at Jhelum River, Kashmir

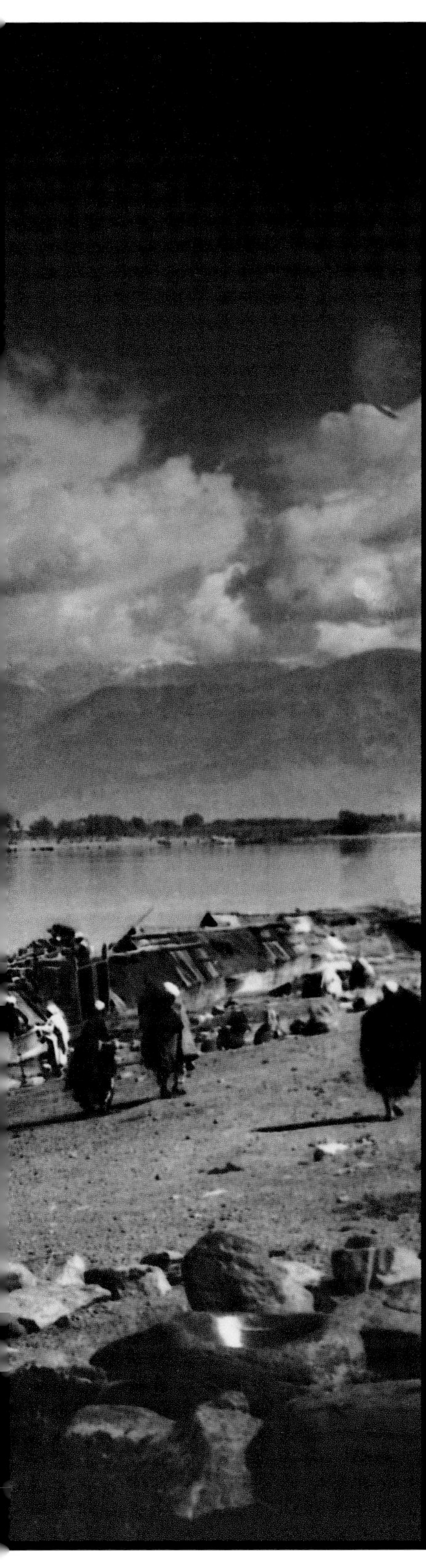

One name that cast a magic spell on me in the early thirties, when I was a teenager just starting to take interest in pictorial photography, was Abid Mian Lal Mian Syed. I saw the original print of Traveller of the East exhibited at the first All-India Salon of Photography, organised by the Photographic Society of Bangalore in 1936.

In his photographs of the Kashmir Valley, the clouds fit into the landscapes so admirably that I could not resist the temptation of asking him, when I first met him in Delhi in 1951, whether he carried the clouds in his kit bag and let them loose to fill up a blank sky. It is a sad thought that India has not produced another Syed.

T Kasinath
New Delhi

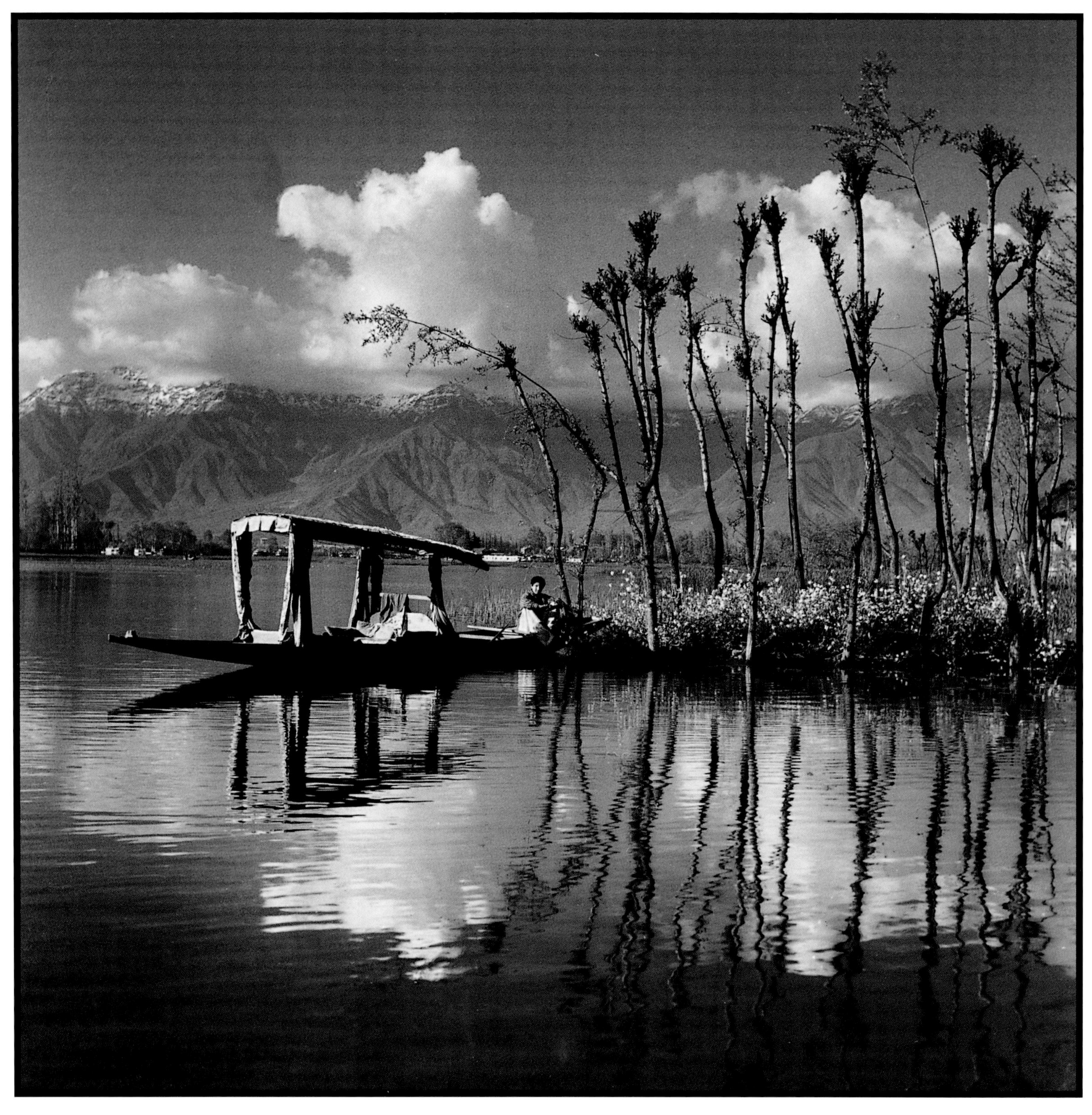

Monsoon evening at Dal Lake, Kashmir

Right: Palanpur House, Mount Abu

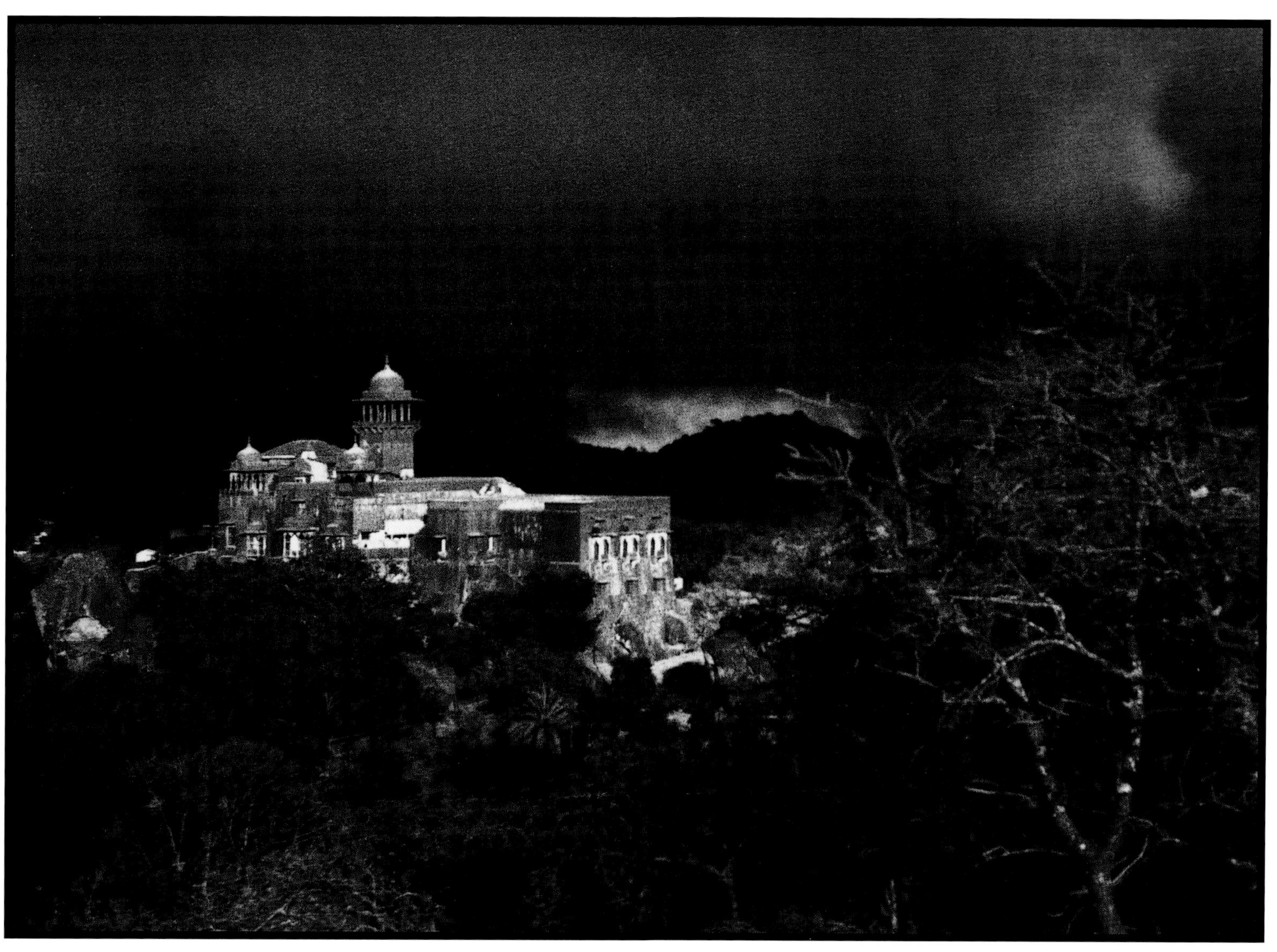

Apart from his professional pursuits, Mr. A L Syed was a great humanitarian and every inch a gentleman. I knew him as my patient and I would say he excelled in all spheres of life. He was truly a man to remember. I wish a memorial of A L Syed would be constructed to inspire and guide the future generation of photographers. May this book go a long way in serving the art of photography in our country.

Dr. B T Trivedi
Former Civil Surgeon, Palanpur

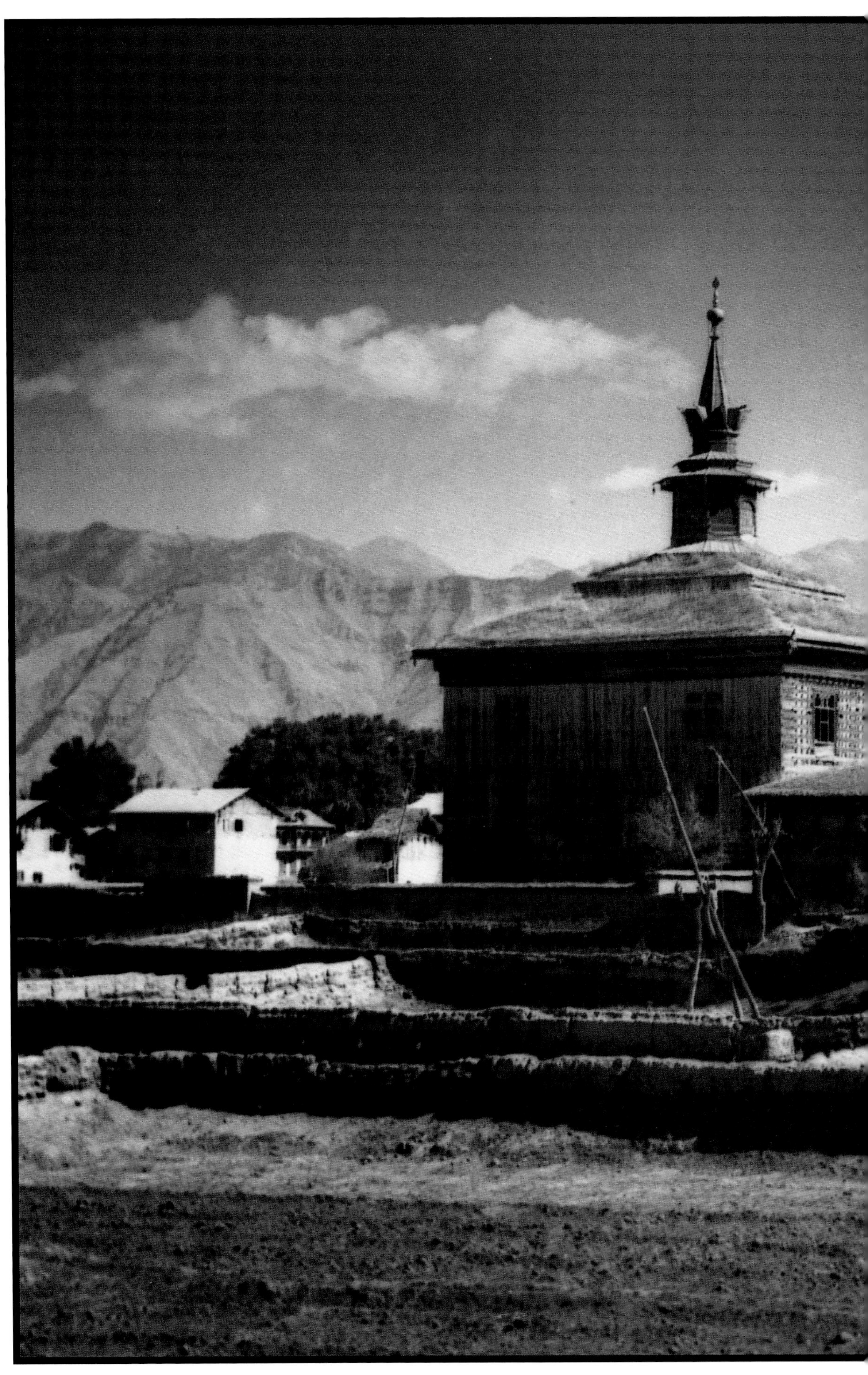

In old Nepal

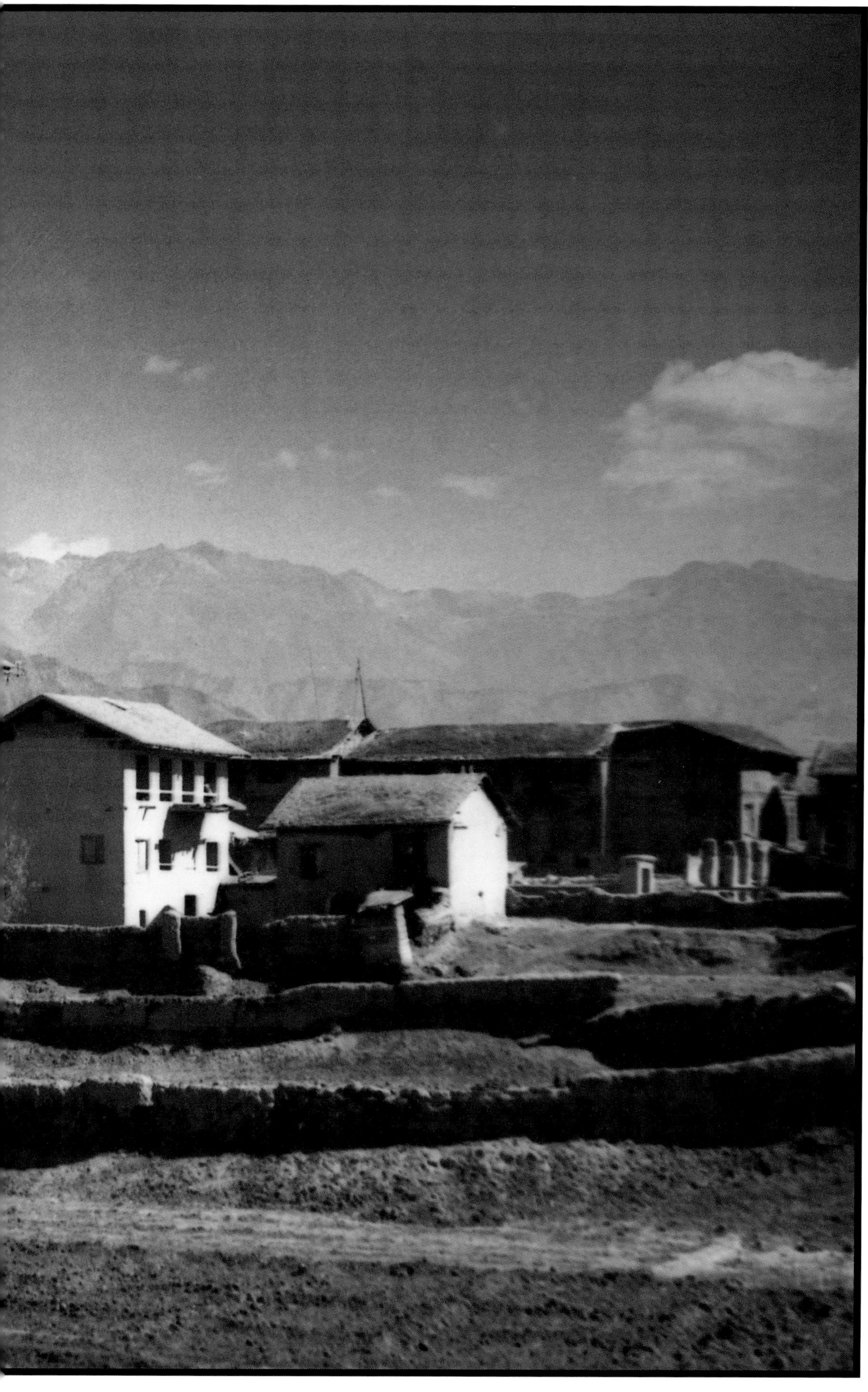

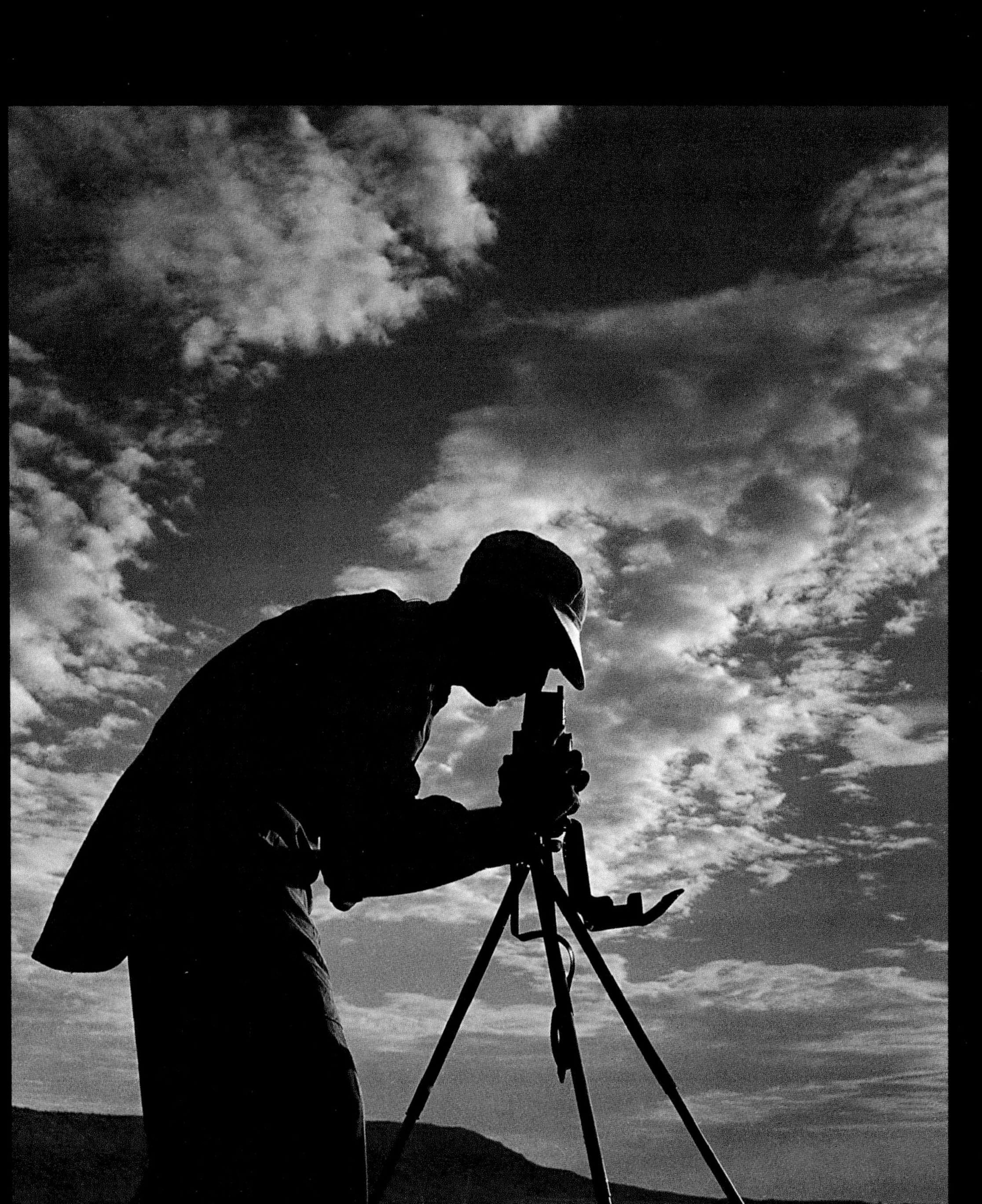